The Broadsheet Melbourne Cookbook

A book by Broadsheet
Photography by Mark Roper
Art Direction and Design by The Company You Keep

BROADSHEET MEDIA

plum. Pan Macmillan Australia

Broadsheet is Australia's leading independent online magazine and directory, covering life, culture and style. A hub for people who love to get involved in city life, Broadsheet keeps readers in the know about the best of what each city has to offer. This collection of Melbourne's most iconic recipes, hand-selected from its best restaurants, cafes and bars – from the big names to neighbourhood gems – is the definitive guide to where and what to eat in Melbourne.

The Broadsheet Melbourne Cookbook

Featuring:

400 Gradi
5 & Dime
A1 Bakery
Añada
Baker D. Chirico
Bar Di Stasio
The Beaufort
Blackhearts & Sparrows
The Brûlée Cart
Brunswick Street Alimentari
Builders Arms Hotel
Burch & Purchese Sweet Studio
Cheerio
Chez Dré
Chin Chin
Cibi
Cicciolina
Cobb Lane
Coda
Cumulus Inc.
Cutler & Co.
Dainty Sichuan
David's Restaurant
Dench Bakers
DOC Pizza & Mozzarella Bar
Duchess of Spotswood
Epocha
Estelle Bistro
The European
The Everleigh
The Farm Cafe
Five Points Deli
France-Soir
Fukuryu Ramen
Gerald's Bar
Hammer & Tong 412
Hardware Société
Horn Please
HuTong Dumpling Bar
Huxtaburger
I Love Phở
Izakaya Den
Jinda Thai
Kaprica
The Kettle Black
Ladro
Le Bon Ton
Little Bertie
Lune Croissanterie
Mamasita
The Merchants Guild
Mixed Business
Monsieur Truffe
MoVida
N. Lee Bakery Cafe
Pei Modern
Philippa Sibley
Pidapipó
Pierre Roelofs
Pope Joan
The Premises
Rockwell and Sons
Rumi
Small Batch
Small Victories
Supermaxi
Supernormal
T. Cavallaro & Sons
Téta Mona
Tomboy
Tonka
The Town Mouse
Tuck Shop Take Away
Twenty & Six Espresso
Umberto Espresso Bar
Vue de Monde
Yong Green Food

Chez Dré, South Melbourne

Contents

→

Lunch

Dinner

→

Dessert

Chez Dré, South Melbourne

Foreword
by Andrew McConnell, Chef

In the last eight or so years the food and beverage industry in Melbourne has experienced this incredible ascent. When Broadsheet landed here, it anchored itself squarely in the middle of all of that and created its own niche. In no time at all, Broadsheet became a reference point for everything that was happening in Melbourne, having this great knack of having its foot in the door before the door was even open.

Our customers today eat out more often and know so much about what they're eating. They're in tune with what's happening. There's no doubt that the industry has changed in sync with how people want to eat out – it's responding to the environment, and so is Broadsheet with this cookbook.

In my experience, good recipes have long life cycles and will be just as accepted or approachable in ten years as they are today, but it can be nice to reminisce as well. Because our industry is quite trend-influenced it will be interesting to look back at what we were eating at the time this cookbook was published, the same way it's good fun for me to look at old menus.

I'm motivated to cook because I'm a chef and I enjoy the industry. I love cooking in Melbourne and being a Melburnian, but most importantly I get a lot of satisfaction from the creative process of cooking and sharing. That's what drives me, and hopefully The Broadsheet Melbourne Cookbook brings joy to others in the same way.

Introduction

Since our earliest days, when a single pair of hands delivered the Broadsheet paper to a dozen cafes, Melbourne's dining culture has changed in extraordinary ways.

Our changing hospitality landscape is fascinating, but just as interesting is the transformation of our own relationship with food. Eating at cafes and restaurants has become so commonplace that the exception is no longer dining out; it's dining in.

'Cooking is such a wonderful form of creativity, such a wonderful assault on the senses. It's the ultimate form of socialising,' says Kate Bartholomew, owner of Coda and Tonka.

People such as Bartholomew, and the many Melbourne chefs and restaurateurs who helped bring this book to life, have created a food culture that in a few short years has turned our approach to dining on its head.

There's a reason we snap our coffee before we sip it, line up to squeeze next to another couple at Mamasita and set our alarms earlier on a Saturday than during the week for a croissant at Lune. Food is our common ground. Regardless of who you are or where you've come from, you have to eat. And while you might as well enjoy it, it's a privilege to understand it. What better way to understand than to recreate these experiences at home?

The motivation to cook is often found beyond our own kitchens, and there is little that inspires us more than the creativity of our cafes and restaurants.

The Broadsheet Melbourne Cookbook is our tribute to the city's rich culinary culture, a collection of recipes from some of our best cafes, restaurants and bars. The people behind them are our tastemakers, our innovators, and this book is our way of connecting the dots between a restaurant's philosophy and what ends up on our plates.

Andrew Kelly, owner of Small Batch Roasting Co., Counter, Filter and Auction Rooms, believes Melbourne's hospitality operators have created a self-propelling cycle, where constant innovation leads to constant advancements. Key to this rise in standards, Kelly says, is the increased awareness of where produce originates.

'St Ali emerged doing in-shop roasting, and starting to source direct from individual producers. This inspired others, who tried to do the same or something better,' Kelly says. 'It's been happening over the past ten years, this kind of upping of the ante. It's led to people trying to do more and more and be better and better.' For Kelly, this momentum, the way our cafes and restaurants inspire each other, is an intensely exciting part of the equation. It is, he says simply, 'what's special about Melbourne.'

It may have started with establishments such as St Ali, but we hope this momentum carries into your kitchen. To help, the chef or restaurateur responsible for each

Coda, Melbourne

Kaprica, Carlton

recipe in this book has given us some insight into what makes these dishes sing. All agreed that the key is to be found in taking advantage of quality ingredients.

Of course, this is nothing new. In restaurants, good, locally sourced ingredients have become an expectation, where previously they were a selling point. 'I fundamentally feel that connection to produce is part of a good life – understanding where something has come from while supporting people doing humble work,' says Kelly, who shows us how to make filter coffee at home on page 21. 'It's such a connected way to live.'

There's no reason not to adopt the same philosophy at home. Kelly suggests that in the long run, building relationships with suppliers – the same way a restaurant does – will translate into time saved when choosing what to cook and the bonus side effect of producing unbeatable results at the dinner table. He suggests starting at a farmers' market, where trusted suppliers come together in one location.

Ultimately, The Broadsheet Melbourne Cookbook is a celebration of our diverse culinary landscape – from the big names to the neighbourhood gems – in what is a new format for us. Distilling Melbourne's restaurant scene into 80-odd recipes was no easy task, but the cultures and cuisines we've included can be seen as a representative sample of the entire city.

The Broadsheet Melbourne Cookbook is structured by breakfast, lunch, dinner and dessert, with drinks in between, but that's not to say you can't eat black sticky rice for dessert as well as breakfast, or dumplings any time you feel the craving.

Between sections, some of the city's experts walk us through the fundamentals, be they baking sourdough from scratch or choosing wine to match everything from breakfast dishes to fried chicken.

In a way, the recipes in this book have been chosen by you. Restaurant and cafe owners told us repeatedly that many of these dishes remain fixtures on their menus for fear of public uproar should they ever be removed.

'Most cookbooks, of course, only cover one restaurant, but The Broadsheet Melbourne Cookbook is a cross-section of everything great about Melbourne's food scene,' says Chris Lucas, the restaurateur behind Chin Chin (see page 88), Baby Pizza, Kong BBQ and Hawker Hall. 'Broadsheet has a fresh and special vision that understands today's culture in food. It brings a unique sense of Melbourne style and captures the city's energy.'

We never envisioned that in one decade, Melburnians' emotional connection to food would increase as it has. A big part of that lies in the stories behind every plate, whether those are about local chefs leading global innovation, or a family's new start in a foreign country. The Broadsheet Melbourne Cookbook gives you the opportunity to celebrate Melbourne's rich restaurant culture in your own home, on your own terms. More than that, it's a celebration of the everyday importance of dining well.

Cibi, Collingwood

Breakfast

→

Chez Dré, South Melbourne

3–9 Little Howard Street
North Melbourne

Making Filter Coffee
with Andrew Kelly of Small Batch

You will need

a pour-over cone (1, 2 or 3 cup)

paper filters

jug, large cup or similar

teaspoon

timer

scales

kettle

burr grinder

21g coffee beans

350g water

'You don't need to be a connoisseur to enjoy filter coffee,' says Andrew Kelly, owner of Small Batch Roasting Co., Filter, Counter and Auction Rooms cafe. 'Filter coffee (in this case pour-over) is so simple to make at home,' he says, insisting that you don't need to pour water anticlockwise from a fancy Japanese pouring kettle to make a decent filter. The equipment will cost you around the price of four coffees and it involves adding water to ground beans. The standard brew ratio for making filter coffee is 60–70 grams of coffee per litre of water, depending on the size of your grind and how strong you like your coffee. At home, Kelly uses a scalable version of the recipe; around 21 grams of coffee in 350 grams of water, which is enough to serve two people in small cups with refills (those who prefer a stronger brew can up it to 22 grams). Kelly uses a 2-cup pour-over cone, which will make between one and three cups, and recommends using a set of scales to precisely measure your coffee versus water ratio.

Set up the cone

While you wait for the kettle to boil, place the filter paper in your pour-over cone and position it directly on top of or above your cup or jug. Pour boiling water around the edges of the filter to rinse it. The water will drop into the vessel, both cleaning your filter and warming your cone and cup. Discard the water.

→

Grind the beans

Brew your coffee within 30 minutes of grinding your beans. Kelly suggests using a burr grinder instead of a blade grinder for an even grind. Make sure it's a medium grind, slightly coarser than for an espresso. Place the ground beans into the middle of the filter paper. They will form a 'coffee bed'.

Make a coffee bed

Start the timer and pour about 60g of your nearly-boiling water onto the coffee bed, ensuring that every granule is evenly saturated. Stir thoroughly and allow it to rest for half a minute. This process is called 'blooming'. Add the rest of the water (until you have 350g total) over another 30–45 seconds. Pour in a roughly circular motion, wetting all of the surface area of the coffee while avoiding pouring on the side of the cone itself. If your coffee bed is thick and dry when you begin to pour, stir it a little to help incorporate the water and coffee.

Stir it

After all of the water has been poured into the cone, settle the coffee bed by lifting the cone and lightly tapping it once or twice on top of the cup or jug below. Take your teaspoon and make a couple of circular motions around the top of the water line in the cone to create a slight vortex. The remaining water should take about 2½–3 minutes to fully drain through the coffee, depending on the volume being brewed.

Drink it

When there is no longer any water visible upon the surface of the coffee bed, it's ready to drink. Before serving, swirl it around a little. Kelly insists on leaving milk out of the picture. 'Just drink it as it is. It's sweet, there are often perceptible fruit, herbal, floral, candied nut and chocolate or toffee flavours,' he says. 'You'll taste it change as it cools.'

202 Bellair Street
Kensington

Bircher Muesli with Coconut Labna and Berry Compote
The Premises

Serves 6

4 cups rolled oats

⅓ cup sultanas

⅓ cup chopped dates

⅓ cup shredded coconut

½ green apple, grated and tossed with 1 tablespoon lemon juice

700ml cloudy apple juice

honey, to serve

toasted coconut, to serve

toasted flaked almonds, to serve

Coconut labna

500g plain yoghurt

200ml coconut cream

3 teaspoons caster sugar

Berry compote

½ cup caster sugar

½ vanilla pod, split lengthways, seeds scraped

1 strip of orange zest

250g strawberries, halved

125g blueberries

125g raspberries

125g blackberries

He's the coffee guy and she runs the kitchen. The Premises, run by couple Alex Anderson and Kate Holloway, is where Kensington locals come for a brunch worth boasting about. But it's simpler dishes, like this Bircher Muesli, that make this cafe stand out from the crowd.

'We use organic oats and don't add sugar,' says Anderson, who eats it every morning. 'It suits the health conscious and it's really achievable to make at home; you don't need fancy techniques, just good-quality ingredients.' In the past the kitchen has altered the Bircher recipe every few months, but Anderson reckons this is the best yet. It can also be pre-prepared and kept in the fridge – ideal for those who prefer an extra 10 minutes in bed in the morning.

This recipe will need to be started the day before serving.

Add the oats, sultanas, dates and shredded coconut to a large bowl and mix well. Add the grated apple and apple juice and stir to combine. Transfer the mixture to an airtight container and refrigerate overnight.

For the coconut labna, line a sieve with muslin and place over a bowl. Tip the yoghurt into the lined sieve and tie the corners of the cloth together. Hang the bundle from a wooden spoon over a deep bowl and refrigerate overnight (or a minimum of 4 hours) for the whey to drain off. Once the yoghurt has been strained, unwrap the parcel and place the labna in a medium bowl. Stir in the coconut cream and sugar. Discard the whey.

For the berry compote, add the sugar, vanilla pod and seeds, orange zest and 250ml of water to a medium saucepan over medium heat. Bring to a simmer and reduce to a light syrup, about 4–5 minutes. Once reduced, add the berries and cook for 6 minutes. Remove from the heat and set aside to cool.

To serve, add some Bircher to each bowl and top with a generous amount of coconut labna and berry compote. Drizzle over some honey and sprinkle with the toasted coconut and flaked almonds.

285–287 Coventry Street
South Melbourne

Pecan and Cranberry Granola
Chez Dré

Serves 5

50g unsalted butter

2 tablespoons honey

1½ tablespoons golden syrup

70g raw sugar

1 pinch of salt flakes

100g rolled oats

65g pecans

½ cup flaked almonds

75g desiccated coconut

1½ tablespoons chopped pistachios

1½ tablespoons dried cranberries

Chez Dré's granola is so popular that the cafe has sent bags of it to interstate visitors who couldn't quell their cravings after tasting it. Inspired by a recipe from the owner's time at the five-star Lanesborough Hotel in London, it's a breakfast simple in assembly but complex in flavour. 'One day I was put on the breakfast shift and I opened up the granola box to the amazing, fresh smell of buttery honey oatiness. How could I resist sticking my hand in to do some "quality control?"' says Andrea 'Dre' Reiss.

She made it her own by adding cranberries to counterbalance the sweetness of the honey and golden syrup, and now assembles it at Chez Dré in 10-kilogram batches a couple of times a week. The result is a balance of toastiness, nuttiness, sweetness and tartness. 'It has that home-baked quality that takes you back to your childhood,' says Dre.

Preheat the oven to 110°C fan-forced (130°C conventional). Line a heavy baking tray with baking paper.

Combine the butter, honey, golden syrup, sugar and salt in a small saucepan and warm, stirring, until the sugar has melted – this will stop the sugar crystallising in the granola.

Add the oats, pecans, almonds and coconut to the bowl of a stand mixer and combine using the paddle attachment. If doing this step by hand, you will need to chop the pecans, but the paddle of the mixer will crush them sufficiently. Pour the hot liquid over the dry ingredients and mix until all ingredients are coated. If you're not using a mixer, it is better to actually use your hands to incorporate everything, but wait until the butter syrup cools down, as it will be quite hot.

Spread the mixture out on the prepared tray and bake for 20 minutes. Turn the tray around in the oven and bake for another 20 minutes. Stir the granola regularly to make sure it cooks evenly. To check that the granola is done, take a small amount from the oven and place it on the benchtop. Allow it to cool completely and if it hardens and goes crunchy, then it's ready; if still chewy, continue to cook further.

Once cooked, tip the granola onto a clean benchtop and add the pistachios and cranberries. Mix together and break into chunks with your hands or a metal spoon before it cools completely. Store in an airtight container.

594 Queensberry Street
North Melbourne

Black Sticky Rice with Banana, Mango and Puffed Wild Rice

Twenty & Six Espresso

Serves 6

300g black glutinous rice

1 vanilla pod, split lengthways

1 ripe banana, sliced

100g white sugar

600ml coconut cream

3 ripe mangos, peeled, cheeks sliced off

100g fresh passionfruit pulp (about 10–12 fresh passionfruit)

100g puffed wild rice (raw wild rice quickly fried at 190–200°C and drained on paper towel) or toasted coconut flakes

'We needed to think of a dish that was vegan, dairy free and gluten free,' says Nedin Rahmanovic, the chef behind Twenty & Six's most popular dish. 'I'm a huge fan of rice pudding in general, and I was looking to put it on the menu in a way that was more nourishing than its dessert counterpart.'

Traditionally an English dish made with white rice and a sprinkling of cinnamon, Rahmanovic has given his rice pudding a South-East Asian spin, serving it with black rice, mango, passionfruit pulp and, occasionally, edible flowers. Rahmanovic says you can pick wild edible flowers if you know where to look, or gourmet grocers and Victoria and South Melbourne markets should stock them. In lieu of blooms, puffed rice or toasted coconut flakes can add a wonderful textural element. Grilled pineapple or papaya can also replace the mango, but it's important to use a thick coconut cream to avoid a watery texture and bleeding from the black rice. Try Kara coconut cream for best results.

In a medium saucepan, bring 1 litre of water to the boil. Add the black rice and vanilla pod and cook, uncovered, for 30–35 minutes on a very low heat, stirring only occasionally, until soft and sticky. Drain, remove the vanilla pod and tip the rice into a large bowl.

Add the banana and sugar to the bowl with the rice and mix until combined.

Divide the coconut cream between the serving bowls and add the rice. Top the rice with the mango (either as whole cheeks wedged into the rice, or sliced into three pieces each and crisscrossed on top) and passionfruit pulp and sprinkle over the puffed rice or coconut flakes.

29 Scott Street
Elwood

Almond Croissants
Lune Croissanterie

Makes 10 croissants

½ cup caster sugar

10 x 1-day-old croissants

½ cup flaked almonds

icing sugar, for dusting

Frangipane

250g butter, at room temperature

250g caster sugar

3 eggs

250g almond meal

Followers of Lune's cult-status croissants, listen up: owner Kate Reid is hiding her pastries from you. 'It's true,' she laughs when we ask her. 'Traditionally, in France, leftover croissants are sold the following day filled with an almond frangipane and baked a second time. But at Lune, because we never have any leftover croissants, we have to bake pastries especially and allocate them for the almond croissants.'

After graduating with an Aeronautical Engineering degree and working with Formula One developing cars, Reid realised she wasn't where she wanted to be. She tossed aside that career and studied the art of pastry in Paris. By 2012 she was supplying her flaky, buttery goods to some of Melbourne's best cafes. A year later, she and her brother, Cameron, opened to hoards of people lining up outside their miniscule bakery door in Elwood, some from 4am. They began putting aside 75 croissants each day to ensure the demand was met for these almond pastries, implemented a six-pastry quota to even the stakes for customers and – less than a couple of years later – upgraded to a 400-square-metre warehouse space in Fitzroy. We suggest purchasing as many plain croissants as the quota will allow and trying out this recipe the next day.

Preheat the oven to 180°C fan-forced (200°C conventional). Line a large baking tray with baking paper.

To make the frangipane, beat the butter and sugar on low speed with an electric mixer until light and fluffy, about 2–3 minutes (use a K beater if using a stand mixer). Add the eggs one at a time, waiting until each one is incorporated fully before adding the next. Mix in the almond meal until incorporated and transfer to a piping bag.

To make the sugar syrup, add 250ml of water and the sugar to a small saucepan and stir over medium heat until the sugar has dissolved. Bring the syrup to the boil and take off the heat.

Cut the croissants in half horizontally and brush the cut sides of each croissant generously with the syrup. Pipe a healthy amount of frangipane onto the bottom half of each croissant and sandwich with the top halves. Top each croissant with a piped seam of frangipane and finish with the flaked almonds. Place the croissants on the prepared baking tray and bake for 18–20 minutes until the frangipane is set.

Once cooled, dust the almond croissants with the icing sugar.

Mixed Business, Clifton Hill

Dench Bakers, Abbotsford

218 Swan Street
Richmond

Brioche French Toast with Millionaire Bacon and Banana
Little Bertie

Serves 4

- ⅓ cup brown sugar
- 80ml coconut, olive or peanut oil
- 1 teaspoon ground allspice
- 1 pinch of chilli flakes
- 4 eggs
- 80ml cream
- 12 small bacon rashers
- 2 tablespoons butter
- 8 slices of brioche
- 3 bananas, cut into 1cm slices
- toasted walnuts, to serve
- maple syrup, to serve

A lot of love goes into the bacon at Berties Butcher before it ends up on eggy brioche French toast, flanked by caramelised banana slices and doused in maple syrup. It's cut thick from free-range Berkshire pigs in Wangaratta, where Greta Valley works with a local nutritionist to develop its feed. Berties then has it smoked by one of the original founders of Istra Smallgoods. Chefs buy it by the loin, rashers regularly sell out in store and the cafe out the back, Little Bertie, puts it all over its breakfast menu. 'It's naturally sweet bacon, so it makes sense to pour maple syrup all over it,' says co-owner Darren Moncrieff of the French-toast dish.

Moncrieff is the third operator to run the butcher, but the only one to limit its stock to organic and free-range meats. 'Ten years ago it was hard to find a free-range butcher in Melbourne. Our business is based around free-range meats, the paddock-to-plate element and transparency. The integrity is in the product. That's the big thing,' says Moncrieff. When making this recipe at home, Moncrieff insists you get what you pay for with bacon, so try to buy the unpackaged stuff and always make sure it's Australian.

Combine 2 tablespoons of the sugar and 2 tablespoons of the oil with the allspice and chilli flakes in a medium bowl. Add the bacon and toss to evenly coat.

Beat the eggs and cream in a medium bowl until combined.

Heat two large frying pans over medium heat. Fry the bacon in one pan for 1–2 minutes on each side until cooked to your liking. Melt the butter in the other pan.

Dip the brioche slices in the egg mix, coating both sides well, and fry in the butter for about 1 minute on each side until golden brown and toasted – you will need to do this in batches or have a third pan on the stove.

Mix the remaining oil and sugar in a medium bowl. Add the banana and toss to evenly coat.

Cook the banana in a large frying pan over medium heat for 1½–2 minutes, turning frequently to caramelise evenly and prevent the banana from becoming mushy.

Place two slices of toast on each plate and top with the banana and bacon. Scatter over some walnuts, drizzle with the maple syrup and serve.

617 Rathdowne Street
North Carlton

Buttermilk Waffles with Gingerbread Ice Cream, Toasted Marshmallow, Pumpkin Custard, Pecans and Maple Syrup

Small Victories

Serves 4

Gingerbread

175g brown sugar

150g plain flour

⅓ teaspoon baking powder

2 teaspoons ground cinnamon

½ teaspoon ground ginger

½ teaspoon ground nutmeg

⅛ teaspoon ground cloves

⅛ teaspoon ground white pepper

¼ teaspoon salt flakes

75g cold butter, diced

1 small egg, beaten

→

Terms such as 'house-made' have become buzzwords in cafe culture, but crafting everything from scratch is what sets the guys at Small Victories apart. That includes making butter, yoghurt and all the cafe's meat products – 'Everything apart from rearing the animals,' says co-owner Ben Farrant.

That same logic applies to these waffles. With five separate recipes involved (one for the buttermilk waffles and four for the decadent toppings), they're not something you make every day. 'Maybe you'd make them for an Easter weekend breakfast or a fancy get-together, or perhaps when you want to impress a certain lady or certain guy,' says chef Alric Hansen, who looked to America when concocting the recipe. 'The reference was autumn; pumpkin pie, s'mores and stuff like that. The pumpkin custard is basically pumpkin-pie filling.'

The dessert-like additions of gingerbread, marshmallow and ice cream can also be made and enjoyed separately. Although Hansen tastes every batch, he doesn't have a sweet tooth and claims to be more of a 'blueberry, bananas and chia seeds' guy. 'It takes a certain person to eat waffles like this for breakfast,' he says.

You will need a candy thermometer, an ice cream machine, a blowtorch and a waffle maker for this recipe.

Preheat the oven to 170°C fan-forced (190°C conventional).

For the gingerbread, sift the dry ingredients into a large bowl and make a well in the centre. Add the butter and, using your hands, rub through the flour mixture until an even sand-like consistency. Add the beaten egg and cut through with a butter knife until just combined. Form into a block and refrigerate for 30 minutes.

Once rested, remove the dough from the fridge and sandwich between two sheets of baking paper. Roll out until 5mm thick, remove the top sheet of paper and slide onto a baking tray. You will only need about a quarter to a third of the cooked gingerbread for the ice cream, so you can either cut it into shapes now, or freeze excess dough wrapped in baking paper and foil for another time. Bake for about 15 minutes until golden. Set aside to cool. Store in an airtight container until needed.

→

Gingerbread ice cream (makes 1.5 litres)

- 500ml double cream
- 500ml full-cream milk
- 7 egg yolks
- 250g caster sugar
- 2 teaspoons ground ginger

For the ice cream, place a large bowl in the refrigerator ready to cool the custard.

Gently heat the cream and milk in a medium saucepan until just under the boil.

Meanwhile, whisk the egg yolks and sugar in a large bowl until pale.

When the cream mixture is hot, gradually pour into the yolk mixture while whisking. Once combined, strain back into the pan over medium heat. Using a heatproof spatula, stir constantly and thoroughly until 78°C. As soon as the temperature is achieved, remove from the heat and stir in the ground ginger. Pour through a clean sieve into the chilled bowl and refrigerate, stirring occasionally, until cool.

Meanwhile, break some of the cooled gingerbread (you will need 100g of crushed gingerbread for the ice cream) up into smaller pieces and wrap in a tea towel. Using a rolling pin, crush until quite fine.

Once the custard has cooled, pour into an ice cream machine and churn following the manufacturer's instructions. When almost ready, add the gingerbread crumb to the ice cream. Continue churning for a few more minutes. Take the ice cream out of the churn and place in the freezer in an airtight container.

Vanilla marshmallows (makes about 35)

- 10 gold-strength gelatine leaves
- 400g caster sugar
- 92g liquid glucose
- 1 pinch of salt flakes
- 150ml water
- 1 vanilla pod, split lengthways, seeds scraped
- 200g egg whites (about 7 eggs)
- 50g cornflour
- 50g icing sugar

For the vanilla marshmallows, bloom the gelatine by placing it in iced water until softened, about 5 minutes.

Add the sugar, glucose, salt, vanilla seeds and 150ml of water to a medium saucepan over medium heat, stir to combine and heat until the mix reaches 120°C.

Meanwhile, beat the egg whites with an electric mixer on low speed until foamy.

When the temperature of the syrup is reached, take the pan off the heat and add the gelatine once squeezed of excess water. Using a heatproof spatula, carefully stir until incorporated.

Slowly pour the syrup in a steady stream into the egg whites while whisking. When all the syrup has been added, increase the mixer to full speed and continue to whisk for 10–15 minutes until thick, glossy and lukewarm.

Combine the cornflour and icing sugar in a small bowl. Tip into a fine sieve and apply a fine even layer over a 20cm x 30cm tray. Pour the marshmallow mix onto the tray and smooth the surface with an offset palette knife. Sieve a coating of the icing sugar mix over the top of the marshmallow and cool at room temperature for at least 4 hours before cutting.

Turn the cooled marshmallow out onto a board and, using the icing sugar mix to coat the knife blade, cut into squares. Dust with more sugar mix and store in an airtight container for up to 2 weeks.

Caramelised pumpkin custard (makes about 1 litre)

- 1kg peeled pumpkin, roughly cubed
- 2 eggs
- 1 egg yolk
- 250ml double cream
- ½ cup brown sugar
- ⅓ cup caster sugar
- ½ teaspoon salt flakes
- 2 teaspoons ground cinnamon
- 1 teaspoon ground ginger
- ¼ teaspoon ground nutmeg
- ¼ teaspoon ground cloves
- ¼ teaspoon ground cardamom

For the caramelised pumpkin custard, preheat the oven to 180°C fan-forced (200°C conventional). Lightly oil a baking tray.

Place the pumpkin on the prepared tray and roast for about 45 minutes until soft and caramelised. Set aside to cool.

Add 500g (this will be most of it, as it will have lost considerable water while roasting) of the roasted pumpkin and the remaining ingredients to a large, robust jug and blend until smooth with a hand-held blender.

Place the mixture in a saucepan over medium heat and cook until 70°C. Refrigerate in an airtight container until cool. (This will make more custard than you will need for this recipe, and you can halve it if preferred – omit the yolk, use 1 large egg and halve all other ingredients – but you can also bake the leftover custard in a blind-baked sweet pastry case for a simple pumpkin pie.)

Buttermilk waffles

- 2 eggs, separated
- 250g plain unbleached flour
- 1 tablespoon baking powder
- 2 teaspoons caster sugar
- 1 pinch of salt flakes
- 375ml buttermilk
- 115g butter, melted and cooled slightly

For the buttermilk waffles, whisk the egg whites to stiff peaks and refrigerate.

Sift the dry ingredients together into a large bowl. Mix in the buttermilk and egg yolks, then working quickly, mix in the melted butter. Add a third of the whipped egg white to the batter and mix in gently until combined. Add the remainder of the egg white and fold through.

Cook the batter in the waffle maker according to the manufacturer's instructions.

To serve

- toasted pecans
- maple syrup
- mint leaves

To serve, place two waffles on a plate, top with 3 tablespoons of pumpkin custard and three marshmallows. Use a blowtorch to toast the marshmallows and top with a scoop of gingerbread ice cream, a few toasted pecans, a drizzle of maple syrup and a few mint leaves.

50 Albert Road
South Melbourne

Poaching Eggs
with Jesse McTavish of The Kettle Black

You will need

- water
- a large pot
- good-quality white vinegar or lemon juice
- salt
- free-range eggs

Jesse McTavish knows a thing or two about poaching eggs. He's co-owner and executive chef at Top Paddock in Richmond, The Kettle Black in South Melbourne and Higher Ground in the CBD. He races through 20,000 eggs a month at The Kettle Black, while Top Paddock goes through a whopping 35,000 eggs. McTavish uses Villa Verde egg merchants, who source the best eggs from young chickens at free-range farms. While he's volunteered to demystify the secrets behind perfect poaching, McTavish acknowledges the home cook doesn't have access to Villa Verde. Instead, he suggests heading to your local farmers' market and getting to know the person behind the eggs. 'Create relationships with your producers the same way I do; talk to the farmer, ask them if their eggs are from younger, healthier chickens, and how many are on their farm,' he says.

Free-range eggs have a richer depth of flavour and a more vibrant colour, while those laid by younger chooks tend to have a tighter structure, which is visible in the way that the whites hold onto the yolk. This causes a sturdy appearance on the plate with the eggs sitting higher and emerging from the water as more precise domes. It's the easiest way to create that sought-after, rounded poached egg.

The protein in egg whites, called ovalbumin, coagulates with the addition of heat, acid and salt. In other words, it takes on a semi-solid state. This process is sped up by the addition of vinegar and salt to water, heated to between 95°C and 98°C.

→

Heat the water

To achieve a poached egg with a firm, cooked white and a runny yolk, start by adding 5 litres of water to a deep pot. Heat the water to 98°C, then measure out 100ml of vinegar. Add it to the pot, along with a generous pinch of salt. The addition of vinegar lowers the pH level of the water, which in turn speeds up coagulation and results in a smoother appearance for the finished product by preventing the white from forming string-like trails behind the egg. Be sure to use good-quality vinegar, or even lemon juice, to eliminate an overpowering sour taste.

Crack the egg

Take a fresh, 50g egg from the refrigerator and carefully crack it into the pot. The secret is to crack it as close to the water as possible. If you drop the egg in from a height, egg white tails will form. You also risk the yolk bulging out from the white. Cooking too many eggs at a time can cause a drastic change in water temperature and, as a result, inconsistencies in shape. Up to 25 eggs are cooked in a 15-litre pot at The Kettle Black. For your 5-litre pot, don't poach more than eight at a time.

Cook the egg

Leave the egg in the pot for 2 minutes and 45 seconds. Stirring to create a rounder poached egg is a fallacy, so no need to do that. Although it is possible to coagulate eggs at lower temperatures, as seen in cafes serving the popular 60-degree eggs, cooking at a reduced heat results in gelatinous egg whites. Generally, people prefer their whites cooked through and their yolks oozing.

Trim and serve

Remove the egg from the water with a slotted spoon and carefully lay it on an absorbent cloth until the excess water has drained. This will also help remove surplus vinegar. For aesthetic purposes, trim any egg white tails to form a perfectly round poached egg before serving.

Cibi, Collingwood

680 Centre Road
Bentleigh East

Superfood Breakfast
The Merchants Guild

Serves 4

- 1 small head of broccoli, cut into small florets
- ½ cup pumpkin seeds
- 1 cup cooked pearl barley
- 2 cups chopped curly kale
- ½ cup mung bean sprouts
- 1 green chilli, deseeded and finely chopped
- 2 avocados, diced
- 2 tablespoons olive oil
- 1 tablespoon lemon juice
- salt flakes and freshly ground black pepper
- 8 eggs
- 4 slices of sourdough bread
- 300g cottage cheese

'Over my 20 years in the industry, it's incredible to see how differently people are eating now,' says Vincent Conti of The Merchants Guild in Bentleigh. 'So many people are gluten free or can't drink milk. I suppose it's a good thing because people are being more inventive with food ... and it's giving us better options for breakfast. We're using produce that people wouldn't have necessarily thought to include in a breakfast dish.'

True to this healthy focus found on menus around Melbourne is The Merchants Guild's Superfood Breakfast – two perfectly poached eggs and a verdant pile of ingredients tumbling over toast spread with light cottage cheese. It's a crowd favourite among clean eaters and is simple to prepare.

'It's the way people want to dine these days, instead of eating a big breakfast. It's still filling and it's tasty and nutritious,' says Conti.

Blanch the broccoli in boiling salted water for 2 minutes. Drain and refresh under cold water.

Toast the pumpkin seeds in a dry frying pan over low heat, about 3–5 minutes.

Mix the barley, broccoli, kale, mung bean sprouts, chilli, avocado and pumpkin seeds in a large bowl.

Combine the oil and lemon juice to make a dressing and pour over the salad. Season to taste and toss to combine.

Poach the eggs until cooked to your liking.

Toast the bread and spread with the cottage cheese. Pile the salad on the toast, top with the poached eggs, season and serve.

87 Hudsons Road
Spotswood

Duchess of Pork
Duchess of Spotswood

Serves 4

250g pork jowl

250g pork neck

3 pig's tongues

salt flakes and freshly ground black pepper

120ml Madeira

250ml good-quality veal stock

8 eggs

4 slices of sourdough bread (Duchess of Spotswood uses Zeally Bay)

butter, to serve (Duchess of Spotswood uses Pepe Saya)

fresh truffle, to serve

The most popular dish at Duchess of Spotswood is the Duchess of Pork: crispy pig's jowl on toast with fried eggs and truffled Madeira sauce. When the cafe opened in 2010 in Spotswood, there wasn't much else around. Thanks to a community-oriented attitude and the menu's interesting, English-style breakfast dishes, the Duchess has built its reputation as an iconic destination cafe in the west.

'We put the Duchess of Pork on the menu five years ago, before many of our customers knew what a jowl was,' says co-owner Bobby Green. 'People were asking, "what's jowl?" and I would explain, "it's face; you're eating the face of a pig". We were amazed at how well it sold.' The Duchess of Pork quickly became the cafe's signature dish. Regulars order it without looking at the menu.

This recipe will need to be started 2 days before serving.

Add all the meat to a medium bowl. Prepare enough brine to cover the meat by dissolving 1 heaped teaspoon of salt per litre of water required. Pour the brine over the meat and refrigerate overnight.

The next day, drain off the brine and rinse the meat. Add to a medium saucepan, cover with water and cook over low heat, skimming the impurities as they rise to the top, until the meat is very tender, about 3 hours.

Remove and discard the skin from the tongues. Shred all the meat by hand, discarding the fat from the jowls. Line a small container with baking paper and press the meat into the base, cover with baking paper and place a weight on top to compress. Refrigerate overnight until set.

Reduce the Madeira by two-thirds in a small saucepan. Add the veal stock and warm through. Season to taste and keep warm.

Lift the set meat out of the container and slice into portions of about 120g each.

To serve, fry the eggs in one frying pan over medium heat. Fry the pork in another pan over high heat until crisp and warmed through.

Toast the bread and spread generously with the butter.

Serve each portion of pork with 50–60ml of sauce, a shaving of truffle, two eggs and a slice of toast.

120 Hardware Street
Melbourne

Baked Eggs with Chorizo, Spiced Tomato Concassé and Black Olives
Hardware Société

Serves 4

- 2 tablespoons extra-virgin olive oil
- 1 small onion, finely diced
- 2 tablespoons smoked paprika
- 1 tablespoon tomato paste
- 200g tomatoes, chopped
- salt flakes and freshly ground black pepper
- 4 small handfuls of baby spinach leaves
- 12 eggs
- 50g chorizo, diced (Hardware Société uses Istra Smallgoods)
- 12 black olives, pitted
- chopped flat-leaf parsley leaves, to serve
- crusty bread or buttered toast, to serve

The Hardware Société's version of baked eggs is a much-talked-about dish. 'You can go out to 50 cafes in Melbourne that serve some interpretation of baked eggs,' says Di Keser, co-owner of the cafe with her husband Will. They make theirs in a cast-iron cocotte, which Di insists makes all the difference.

The cafe does a roaring trade on weekends and the chorizo baked eggs account for 25 per cent of food orders. But there's a lot more to these baked eggs than cast iron; they're about as robust as a breakfast offering gets. Customers dip crusty baguette into spiced tomato concassé, breaking apart the gooey egg yolk lurking beneath the surface, then experience the salty whack of black olives and the tingle of spiced sausage and paprika.

Di recommends home cooks invest in mini Staub cast-iron pots for an authentic recreation of the cafe's baked eggs, but also encourages creative licence – vegetarians can remove the chorizo, leftover passata can be used up and different nuts and varieties of cheese can be substituted or added. 'It's what your imagination makes of it, and also whatever's leftover in the fridge,' she says.

You will need four small (or one large) cast-iron cocottes for this recipe.

Preheat the oven to 220°C fan-forced (240°C conventional).

For the concassé, add the oil to a frying pan over medium heat and cook the onion until softened but without any colour, about 3–4 minutes. Add the paprika and cook for 2 minutes. Add the tomato paste and cook for 2 minutes. Add the tomato, bring to the boil and simmer for 5 minutes. Season to taste.

Preheat the cocottes in the oven for 10 minutes.

Divide the spinach between the preheated cocottes and crack in the eggs (3 per cocotte). Top with the chorizo and olives and add 1½ tablespoons of the concassé to each. As the eggs start to cook in the hot cocottes, use a spoon to pull the egg from the side of the dish so that it falls back into the mix. Take care note to break the yolks. Bake for 5–7 minutes until the whites are firm and the yolks are still runny.

Scatter over some parsley and serve with some crusty bread or buttered toast.

45 Keele Street
Collingwood

Chicken Soboro Bowl
Cibi

Serves 6

Soboro

2 tablespoons olive oil

1kg chicken mince

100g red miso paste

60g ginger, finely grated

100g Japanese or white sugar

3 tablespoons mirin

2 tablespoons cooking sake

1 tablespoon tamari

2 tablespoons white sesame seeds, toasted

rice, to serve

½ cup blanched edamame, to serve

½ cup blanched green beans, cut into 1–2cm pieces, to serve

3 finely sliced radishes, to serve

mizuna sprigs, to serve

Soy eggs

3 tablespoons tamari

1 tablespoon Japanese or white sugar

3cm piece of dried kombu (edible kelp)

6 half-boiled eggs, peeled and cut in half

'We always love to share our childhood experiences and memories of flavours with our customers,' says Megumi Tanaka, who owns Cibi with her husband Zenta.

This Chicken Soboro Bowl is Megumi's take on a classic Japanese meal. 'This is one of the great dishes that our grandmothers and mums used to cook for us in Japan,' she says. 'Traditionally, soboro is made with a combination of chicken mince, egg and some greens (or cooked shiitake mushrooms) layered on rice. The chicken mince is generally cooked with soy, sugar and mirin. In our chicken soboro recipe we've added red miso and lots of ginger to make the flavour more interesting. We also soak half a boiled egg in soy and kombu, instead of using minced egg.'

Megumi suggests using cutlery to mix the ingredients with the rice so that each mouthful contains all the elements of the dish. 'You can use chicken soboro itself [the mince] in other dishes, such as stuffing it into vegetables, with noodles and pastas, or even on toast with some cheese. It's a very handy dish you can freeze and save for a busy day's dinner or lunch.'

For the soy eggs, add the tamari, sugar, kombu and 140ml of water to a small saucepan and bring to the boil. Stir to ensure that the sugar has completely dissolved and set aside to cool. Once the liquid has cooled, add to a container with the boiled eggs. Soak the eggs for 1–2 hours.

For the soboro, heat the oil in a large frying pan over medium heat. Add the mince and fry, stirring occasionally, until almost cooked, about 4 minutes. Add the miso and ginger and mix well. Once the mince is cooked thoroughly, add the sugar, mirin, sake and tamari and mix well. Simmer for about 8–10 minutes. Once cooked, scatter over the sesame seeds.

Serve the soboro on rice, topped with the halved soy eggs, edamame, green beans, radish and the mizuna sprigs.

323 Lennox Street
Richmond

Avocado, Broad Bean, Goat's Cheese and Dukkah on Sourdough
Cheerio

Serves 6

1 bunch of mint

600g podded broad beans (fresh or frozen)

120g frozen peas, thawed

3 avocados, roughly diced

1 long green chilli, finely sliced into rings

150g goat's cheese (Cheerio uses Meredith Dairy)

juice of 1 lemon

1 teaspoon ground black pepper

extra-virgin olive oil

salt flakes (Cheerio uses Maldon brand)

12 slices of good-quality sourdough bread, to serve

butter, to serve

Dukkah

50g pine nuts

50g hazelnuts

50g pistachio kernels

50g white sesame seeds

2 teaspoons cumin seeds

2 teaspoons coriander seeds

50g black sesame seeds

2 teaspoons salt flakes

'This recipe screams summer to us,' says Charlotte Devereux, co-owner of Cheerio with her partner Chris Handley. She's referring to their avocado on toast – a dish that has become as important to Melbourne brunch menus as coffee. Whether smashed with feta, piled high or spread like nature's butter, it's a dish that has come to define our city. And for a small place, Cheerio is a big player in the avocado game. It's not surprising given the couple's collective resume; Handley was partner at Wall Two 80 and Devereux managed Seven Seeds and Batch Espresso for years.

Although available year-round, avocados are at their best in summer. It's Cheerio's personal touches to the dish, such as green chilli, sourdough from Woodfrog Bakery and broad beans, that make its avocado toast one of our favourites in the city. When broad beans and peas aren't in season, Devereux recommends buying frozen. She also recommends keeping an extra-large batch of the house-made dukkah in the pantry. 'It stores really well in a dry, airtight container. I use it all the time on other things; it's delicious on scrambled eggs.'

Should you wish to add a couple of poached eggs, like most Cheerio customers do, see The Kettle Black's guide to poaching eggs on page 41.

Preheat the oven to 160°C fan-forced (180°C conventional).

For the dukkah, toast the pine nuts, hazelnuts, pistachios and white sesame seeds on separate baking trays until lightly coloured and fragrant. It's important to get a good amount of colour on the nuts to release as much flavour as possible, but watch them as they can colour quickly and burn. The sesame seeds will be the quickest (2–3 minutes), followed by the pine nuts (3–4 minutes), pistachios (5–6 minutes) and hazelnuts (8–10 minutes). Set aside to cool.

Rub the roasted hazelnuts in a clean dry tea towel to remove the skins. Don't worry if some of the skin remains.

Toast the cumin and coriander seeds in a dry frying pan over medium heat until lightly coloured and fragrant, about 1–2 minutes. Blitz in a spice grinder, or use a mortar and pestle, and add to a medium bowl.

→

LAZER

Once the nuts have cooled, blitz coarsely in a food processor and add to the bowl with the spices. Add the black sesame seeds and salt and combine. The dukkah will keep well in a dry, airtight container.

Pick the mint leaves into a large bowl of cold water and set aside for 10 minutes. Drain, pat dry with paper towel and tear.

Blanch the broad beans in a large saucepan of boiling water for 3 minutes. Drain, refresh under cold water and remove the skins.

Add the broad beans, peas, avocado, chilli, goat's cheese, mint, lemon juice and pepper to a large bowl, drizzle with some oil, season with salt and combine.

Toast the bread and spread with some butter. Evenly distribute the avocado mix over the bread, allowing two slices per serve. Sprinkle 2 tablespoons of dukkah and a handful of mint leaves over each slice and serve.

Berties Butcher, Richmond

RETAIL
OR
WHOLESALERS.
• PORK GRETA VALLEY
WANGARATTA, VIC
• CHICKEN BANNOCKBURN
VIC
TWITTER
LIKE US ON FACEBOOK
www.facebook.com/bertiesbutcher

486 Queens Parade
Clifton Hill

Sherry-Roasted Swiss Brown Mushrooms with Whipped Chevre, Hazelnut and Herb Salad

Mixed Business

Serves 4

200g chevre (Mixed Business uses Meredith Dairy)

2 tablespoons cream

16 Swiss brown mushrooms, stems trimmed

80ml Pedro Ximénez sherry

salt flakes and freshly ground black pepper

80g hazelnuts

½ head of radicchio, finely shredded

2 generous handfuls of picked soft herbs (parsley, dill, chervil, basil etc.)

8 slices of quality sourdough bread

Herb oil (makes 500 ml)

½ bunch of thyme

½ bunch of rosemary

1 fresh bay leaf

2 garlic cloves, bruised with the back of a knife

500ml extra-virgin olive oil

Dressing

150ml extra-virgin olive oil

2½ tablespoons white wine vinegar

2 thyme sprigs, leaves stripped and finely chopped

½ garlic clove, crushed

salt flakes and freshly ground black pepper

Clifton Hill's Mixed Business cafe is a study in simple dishes done well. It's the Sherry-roasted Swiss Brown Mushrooms with Whipped Chevre, Hazelnut and Herb Salad that first won us over.

According to Tom Crowe, Mixed Business co-owner alongside Lauren Bieber, the secret to its popularity is balance. 'Roasted Swiss brown mushrooms take on a dense, rich, almost meaty flavour when roasted with Pedro Ximénez sherry.' Crowe recommends mint and basil for the herb salad during warmer months and winter lettuce, such as radicchio, when the weather cools down. The cheaper and more abundant herbs are the more likely it is that they're in season.

Preheat the oven to 180°C fan-forced (200°C conventional).

For the herb oil, add the herbs and garlic to a medium saucepan and pour over the oil. Warm through for 5–6 minutes on low heat, being careful not to bring to a simmer. Set aside to cool and infuse. Leftover herb oil will last for up to 2 weeks in the refrigerator. This recipe can be halved, but leftover oil is great for roast vegetables, salad dressings or as a marinade for barbecued meat.

Whip the chevre and cream until light and creamy and set aside.

Place the mushrooms on a baking tray, drizzle liberally with the herb oil and sherry and season well with salt and pepper. Roast for 15–20 minutes until the mushrooms release their juices and start to caramelise. Set the mushrooms aside on the tray to rest and absorb the roasting liquid.

Roast the hazelnuts on a baking tray until golden, about 8–10 minutes. Remove the skins by rubbing in a clean tea towel, and then roughly chop the nuts.

For the dressing, combine all the ingredients in a jar, season well and shake to combine. Leftover dressing will keep for up to 1 week in the refrigerator.

Gently combine the radicchio, herbs and hazelnuts in a large bowl. Add the dressing to taste and toss to combine.

To assemble, toast the sourdough and spread liberally with the whipped chevre. Add two slices of toast per plate, top with the warm mushrooms and the herb salad, drizzle over any remaining roasting juices and serve.

16 Katherine Place
Melbourne

Bagels and Schmears
5 & Dime

Makes 6–8 bagels

oil spray

3 tablespoons malt powder

sesame, poppy, caraway or nigella seeds, salt flakes, oats, quinoa, cinnamon sugar, shredded cheese or anything else you like for topping the bagels

Dough

255g lukewarm water

½ sachet (3g) instant yeast

7g malt powder

10.5g salt

450g unbleached bread flour (you can swap ¼ of the flour for rye, whole wheat or spelt flour)

Schmears

cream cheese

flavourings and fillings of your choice

We're lucky to have Zev Forman. Originally from New Jersey, he met an Australian while working as a tour guide in Israel and followed her back across the Indian Ocean. After cooking at a number of fine-dining establishments, he decided it wasn't for him. 'I wanted food that was less fussy and I really missed bagels, so I started making my own and selling them at farmers' markets,' he says.

Initially he was making 150 bagels in a borrowed kitchen space. Now he's opened a store in the CBD and sells up to 3000 bagels a day. For toppings, Forman reckons you can't go past the simple flavoured cream cheese schmears listed here – his house-made bacon maple cream cheese is a bestseller. But it's his version of the traditional deli-style white fish salad – usually made from smoked fish, cream cheese, celery, dill and lemon – which he insists is the best in the world. Forman's given it an Aussie spin, taking advantage of native ingredients such as saltbush, finger limes and either bass grouper or barramundi. 'If the guys from Russ & Daughters had been in Australia, this is how they would have made it,' he says.

This recipe will need to be started the day before serving.

For the dough, combine the water, yeast and malt powder in the bowl of a stand mixer or a large mixing bowl. Add the salt and flour and mix until it comes together in a stiff dough. Rest for 5 minutes.

Turn the rested dough out onto the benchtop and knead for about 10 minutes until the dough is smooth and a bit tacky. The dough should be quite stiff so this will require some effort by hand; if using a stand mixer simply continue mixing with the dough hook until smooth. Try stretching a bit of dough out between your hands – if you can see light through it before it rips, you have created enough gluten and the dough is ready. Place the dough in an oiled bowl and cover with plastic wrap. Set the dough aside in a warm spot for about 1 hour until doubled in size.

After the dough has risen, knock it back and divide into 6–8 pieces. Forman makes his bagels in the traditional size of 114g, but you can make them any size you like. Shape the bagels by rolling the dough pieces into long ropes, then joining the two ends and rolling them together. Alternatively, you can make them by forming a ball and then sticking your finger through the middle and slowly widening the hole until you reach the desired size. Place the bagels onto a greased tray, mist with some oil and cover with plastic wrap. Refrigerate overnight to prove.

→

The next day, take the bagels out of the fridge about 30 minutes before you intend to bake them.

Preheat the oven to 250°C fan-forced (270°C conventional). Line a baking tray with baking paper.

Bring 5 litres of salted water to the boil in a large saucepan and add the malt powder – the water should taste slightly sweet.

To test if the bagels are ready to be boiled, place one in a bowl of cold water: if it sinks and then rises to the top, it's ready; if it sinks and stays on the bottom, try again after 10 minutes.

Place as many bagels as fit comfortably in one layer in the pan. Poach them on one side for 30–60 seconds, turn and give them the same amount of time on the other side. The bagels should change colour slightly and form a skin. Lift from the water and place on a cooling rack.

Sprinkle on your chosen toppings, arrange on the prepared tray and place in the oven. Turn the oven temperature down to 230°C fan-forced (250°C conventional) and bake for 20 minutes, rotating the tray after 10 minutes. Keep an eye on them, as ovens tend to vary. Cool for at least 30 minutes before eating.

For the schmears, you can whip and flavour cream cheese for the bagels to fit any meal. Take a block of cream cheese, quark, ricotta or any fresh curd and whip on low speed with an electric mixer. Whip for about 30 seconds and scrape down the sides. Give it another 30 seconds and add in desired flavours. Whip for a final 30 seconds to incorporate and you're ready to schmear!

Chop up whatever herbs are fresh in your garden and whip through for a fresh topping, adding capers and salt to taste.

For a sweet treat, add a few tablespoons of fruit jam, lemon curd or salted caramel to the cream cheese, which is great on a cinnamon raisin bagel.

For a very un-American spread, add 1 tablespoon of Vegemite.

For a decidedly not kosher snack, fry off a bit of bacon and leave the fat in the pan. Chop and fry about 5 onions for every 100g of bacon. Cook the onions on low heat until sticky and brown. Chop up the bacon and add it back to the pan. Deglaze the pan with a double shot of espresso. Add a small can of chipotle peppers in adobo sauce and a good swig of maple syrup. Cook the jam down for about an hour until very sticky, adding a little water if dry. Refrigerate until cool, whip through the cream cheese and enjoy.

Smoked trout, capers and sliced red onion also make for a great schmear.

DENCH

109 Scotchmer Street
Fitzroy North

Making Sourdough
with Tony Dench of Dench Bakers

You will need

Starter

1 apple or potato

2 cups wholemeal flour

Sourdough

400g wheat flour

8g salt

150g starter
(see recipe above)

'It takes time. A lot of time and a lot of patience,' Tony Dench insists, of making a sourdough loaf from scratch. He owns Dench Bakers with his father, John, along with Dench Cafe in Fitzroy North and Bread & Jam for Frances in Hawthorn. The pair also run a wholesale operation. Each loaf is crafted at the main bakery premises in Abbotsford in professional baking ovens. 'If your oven is gas or fan-forced, the bread may look a little dull,' he explains. 'This is because the steam has dried out and the dough can't expand and caramelise properly.' Still, he agrees there is little more rewarding than baking your own sourdough loaf. Here, Dench shares his instructions on how to make a sourdough starter (the combination of flour and water that ferments to create the yeast necessary for baking sourdough) and subsequently, a loaf. Trial and error is the key here, as baking differs in varied conditions.

Make a sourdough starter from scratch

The starter will need to be made up to 2 weeks before baking.

Boil an organic apple or potato until soft inside when poked with a skewer. Place it in a bowl, cover with plastic wrap and set aside in a warm place out of the sun for a week. After this time it should start to ferment, with bubbles exuding from under the skin. Put on rubber gloves and strip the skin and seeds, then squish it between your fingers to make a pulp. Place the pulp, 1 cup of tepid tap water and 1 cup of organic wholemeal flour into a 2-litre bucket. Mix well and leave covered with plastic wrap for a day. The mix should start to bubble and show signs of fermenting.

This can take 12 hours or 2 days depending on the conditions. When the bubbles stop generating and the mix starts to look flat, it's time to 'feed' your starter again with another cup of wholemeal flour and cup of tepid tap water.

→

Feed the starter

As the bucket starts to fill over successive days, start tipping out a third of the mix prior to feeding. As the ferment gets stronger, tip out half before mixing and start adding 1 ½ cups each of water and flour instead of 1 cup. Repeat this process for at least 2–3 weeks, longer if you can. The time taken for the starter (aka levain, leaven, ferment, sourdough, chef) to ferment and bubble will decrease until it is going through a cycle of feeding, fermenting and becoming flat within around 4–6 hours, depending on your conditions and chosen flour (rye is very quick, wheat is slower, for example). This cycle is your indication that the starter is strong and able to make a good loaf of bread.

Prepare the starter for baking

If you want to re-use your starter, mix it again with the same measurements of flour and water and let it rest for an hour on the bench. Then put it in the fridge and leave it for 1–2 weeks. To re-use, remove it from the fridge the day before baking, let it warm up naturally and then mix in more flour and water. Leave it to ferment overnight and then feed it again. Now you can bake with it. Follow this process after baking and your starter will last forever.

→

CIABATTA LARGE.
CIABATTA SMALL.
SUPER SEED.
LIGHT RYE
.... OF ....
.... OF ....
.... OF ....
.... OF ....

Make the dough

Combine the flour, salt, 250ml of tepid water and starter in a bowl, mix until incorporated and leave to rest for 10 minutes. Tip the contents onto a lightly floured bench and knead it with your hands for 3 minutes, rolling the dough out flat and folding it back into a ball. Your dough should be firm but elastic. Add a touch more water if it feels stiff. Note that it's always easier to add extra flour to a wet dough than vice versa.

Prove the dough

Wrap the dough in a clean, damp tea towel and rest for 10–15 minutes. Knead it again a few more times, for 1 minute or less, before covering it with the tea towel again and allowing it to rest for 1 hour. Be sure to place the dough away from draughts and cold, ideally somewhere reasonably warm, in a plastic bowl. After resting, the dough should begin to prove (become slightly puffy and airy).

Rest the dough

Place the dough back onto a lightly floured bench, kneading it a few times and then sculpting it into your preferred shape: a ball, short Vienna or longer stick. Make a seam on the bottom of the loaf by tightening the dough with your hands. Keep the seam facing upwards and place the loaf-to-be in a floured tea towel, either in a bowl for round shapes or rolled into the tea towel for longer loaf shapes. Rest it for another 1–2 hours.

Check the dough

Your dough should look smooth and even before baking.
→

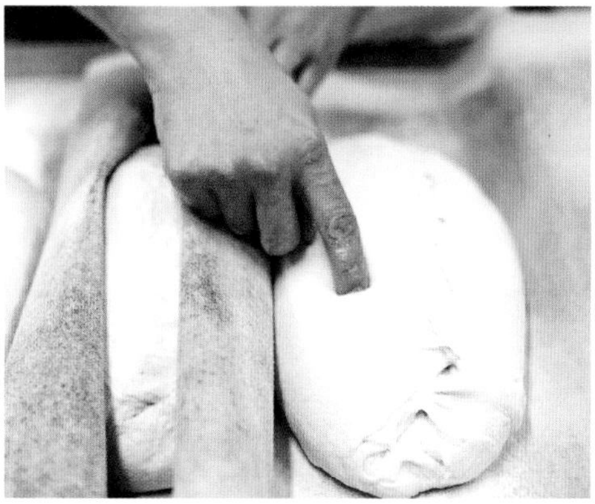

Test the dough

Preheat the oven to 200°C fan-forced (220°C conventional), preheating for at least an hour. Getting the temperature right can be difficult as each oven is different. Trial and error is often the way to go. Test to see if your dough is ready to be baked by lightly poking it. If your finger leaves an indent that doesn't rebound, it is. You'll notice the contrast if you try this step earlier on during proving.

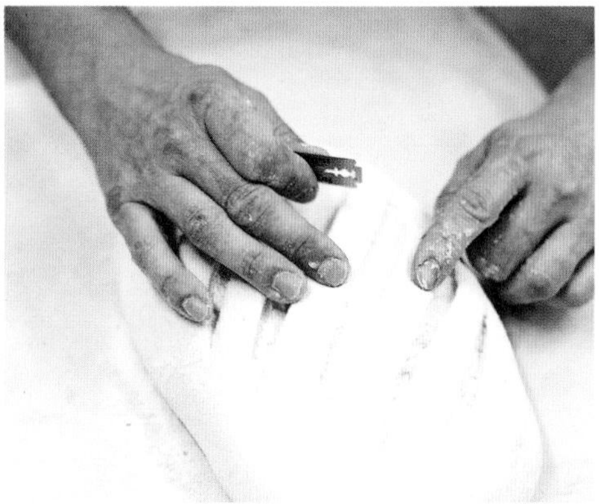

Score the dough

Turn the dough upside-down so the seam is on the bottom and then cut or score it with a pattern using a sharp knife or razor (try one slice lengthways, several cuts across, crosshatching or stripes).

Bake the bread

Place the loaf on a pizza stone or baking tray. Spray the inside of the oven with a water spritzer, put your loaf in and close the door. It should take about 30–40 minutes to bake and turn golden in colour. When ready, the loaf should sound hollow when tapped on the base. If it colours or burns too quickly, your oven is too hot. Try dropping it by 15°C to 20°C next time, but keep the baking time the same.

Builders Arms Hotel, Fitzroy

Lunch

→

Brunswick Street Alimentari, Fitzroy

18 St Heliers Street
Abbotsford

Super Salad
The Farm Cafe

Serves 4

1 cup quinoa, well washed

salt flakes and freshly ground black pepper

2 carrots, grated

1 beetroot, peeled and grated

1 handful of mint leaves, chopped

1 handful of flat-leaf parsley leaves, chopped

2 handfuls of salad greens (spinach, rocket, snow pea shoots etc.)

1½ tablespoons pomegranate molasses

1½ tablespoons extra-virgin olive oil

1 avocado, quartered lengthways

70g toasted pumpkin seeds

Cashew mayonnaise

155g raw cashews, soaked in water for 2 hours

2 pitted dates, soaked in water for 2 hours

¼ cup chopped cauliflower

3 tablespoons extra-virgin olive oil

3 tablespoons lemon juice

1 teaspoon dijon mustard

1 teaspoon apple cider vinegar

¼ teaspoon salt flakes

The Farm Cafe started as a coffee machine in the boot of owners Pip and Tom Hay's car. Now it's an idyllic country-in-the-city retreat where customers tuck into wholesome dishes such as the Super Salad.

'We're aware there are lots of really schmick cafes out there doing amazing restaurant-style cafe food, but we like to keep it to everyday food you can always eat. I have the Super Salad every time we eat there,' says Pip.

'We really like to be seasonal, but with avocado it's sometimes difficult; Melburnians like eating avocado all year around. I think this salad would also be good with some sort of fried cheese. Or I use egg as an avocado substitute,' she says.

Add the quinoa, 375ml of water and a pinch of salt to a medium saucepan and bring to the boil. Reduce the heat to very low, cover and simmer for 10–15 minutes until all the water has been absorbed. Fluff the quinoa with a fork and refrigerate until cool.

For the mayonnaise, drain the cashews and dates and place in a blender or food processor with 125ml of water and the other ingredients. Blend for several minutes until smooth and creamy, adding more water if necessary.

Add the carrot, beetroot, herbs, greens, quinoa, pomegranate molasses and oil to a large bowl, season to taste and toss to combine. Divide the salad between four bowls and top with the avocado, a generous spoonful of cashew mayonnaise and a scattering of pumpkin seeds.

251 Brunswick Street
Fitzroy

Cauliflower and Tahini Salad
Brunswick Street Alimentari

Serves 6–8

vegetable oil, for deep-frying

2 cauliflowers, cut into florets, stalk discarded

1 cup chopped coriander leaves

1 cup chopped flat-leaf parsley leaves

½ cup toasted pine nuts

3 tablespoons currants, soaked in water for 10–15 minutes and drained

salt flakes and freshly ground black pepper

1 large Lebanese pita, toasted and broken into pieces

Dressing

250g Greek yoghurt

65g tahini

80ml lemon juice

80ml olive oil

'Our fruit and vegetable bill easily exceeds our butcher bill, I can tell you that,' says Linda Jones, co-owner of Brunswick Street Alimentari and Smith Street Alimentari, when asked how much produce they go through for their famous salads. 'The quality has to be good; you can't pretend, it has to be fresh. You can't hide anything with fresh salads and we really take pride in ours.'

The vibrant, Middle Eastern–inspired salads rotate daily and are responsible for the lunch rush at this Fitzroy institution, which hasn't settled down since the Brunswick Street store opened in 1998. The farro salad overleaf is Jones' personal favourite. 'It's just divine and it's lovely no matter how long it's sitting on the table. It's even nice the next day.' says Jones. 'It's actually what turned me onto farro.'

'People love the salads because they're actual meals; they're made with grains and beautiful seasoning and just the right flavours.' Jones also suggests seasoning to taste. 'Feel free to make it your own. I think people get a little bit scared with seasoning sometimes. Don't be; go nuts!'

Heat a deep-fryer or saucepan of oil to 180°C.

Deep-fry the cauliflower in batches until golden, about 1 minute for each batch. Drain on paper towel until cool.

To make the dressing, combine all the ingredients in a small bowl.

Place the cooled cauliflower in a large bowl and pour over the dressing. Add the herbs, pine nuts and currants and season to taste. Mix through, scatter over the bread and serve.

251 Brunswick Street
Fitzroy

Italian Farro, Roasted Almond and Persian Feta Salad
Brunswick Street Alimentari

Serves 6–8

500g farro

150g slivered almonds

100g rocket leaves

100g Persian feta, crumbled

Almond pesto dressing

3 garlic cloves

salt flakes and freshly ground black pepper

¼ cup almonds

1½ cups basil leaves

1 cup grated parmesan

1 pinch of ground nutmeg

250ml olive oil

150ml lemon juice

Preheat the oven to 160°C fan-forced (180°C conventional).

Add the farro to a medium saucepan of cold water over medium heat. Bring to a simmer and cook for 15–20 minutes until tender. Drain and rinse under cold water.

Spread the slivered almonds on a baking tray and roast for about 3–5 until golden. Set aside to cool.

For the pesto, use a mortar and pestle (or food processor) to pound the garlic with a little salt. Add the almonds and basil and pound to a paste. Tip into a medium bowl and add the parmesan, nutmeg, oil and lemon juice. Season to taste and combine.

Lightly toss the farro, rocket, crumbled feta, almonds and pesto dressing in a large bowl. Tip into a serving bowl and serve.

100A Lygon Street
Brunswick East

Fattouch Salata with Tahini
Téta Mona

Serves 4–6

- 2 large wholemeal Lebanese pitas
- 1 cos lettuce, cut lengthways into 2cm strips
- 250g cherry tomatoes, halved
- 2 Lebanese cucumbers, sliced on an angle
- 1 spring onion, finely sliced
- 4 radishes, finely sliced
- ½ bunch of flat-leaf parsley, leaves picked and finely chopped
- 1 teaspoon fine Himalayan salt
- 1 tablespoon sumac
- 80ml lemon juice
- 3 tablespoons extra-virgin olive oil
- 2 tablespoons pomegranate molasses
- pomegranate seeds (when available), to serve

Tahini

- 155g raw sesame seeds
- 2 tablespoons mild olive oil
- 3 tablespoons lemon juice
- fine Himalayan salt

Fattouch (or fattoush) salad is a staple on any mezze table, as is tahini, which is used as a topping and to make other popular dishes, such as baba ganoush. Add these to your repertoire and you'll impress any téta.

Identical twins Antoine and Bechara Taouk named Téta Mona in honour of their grandmother after working at their grandfather's bakery in Preston for years. Opening a restaurant together was the logical next chapter for the boys, who grew up eating téta's food. The menu is a combination of their heritage and a more contemporary diet: simple, fresh and full of flavour. They also cater to vegans. The brothers have added their own spin, too, ditching white flour and sugar in favour of unrefined ingredients. These two recipes exemplify Lebanese soul food meets wholefood.

For the tahini, toast the sesame seeds in a dry frying pan over medium heat, stirring or tossing frequently, until lightly coloured and fragrant, about 5 minutes. Tip onto a large plate or tray to cool. Add the cooled sesame seeds to a food processor and process for 2–3 minutes until a crumbly, sticky paste forms – you can use a mortar and pestle for a chunkier consistency. Add the oil and process for 2 minutes, scraping down the sides as necessary, until a thick and fairly smooth paste forms. Add half the lemon juice and an equal amount of water and process. Add more water and lemon juice until the desired consistency is reached. Season to taste and process until combined. Tahini can be stored in an airtight container in the fridge for 3–4 weeks. Stir well before using.

Preheat the oven to 200°C fan-forced (220°C conventional).

Bake the pita for about 5 minutes until toasted and crisp. Set aside to cool. (You can also cut the pita into 3cm wedges and toast or fry.)

Break the lettuce strips apart into a salad bowl. Add the tomatoes, cucumber, spring onion, radish and parsley and toss gently to combine. Sprinkle over the salt and sumac, pour over the lemon juice and oil and toss gently.

Coarsely crush the pita and scatter over the top of the salad, creating a little mountain in the centre of the salad. Drizzle the pomegranate molasses over the top, scatter over the pomegranate seeds and serve the fattouch with the tahini.

Small Victories, Carlton North

Umberto Espresso Bar, Thornbury

125 Flinders Lane
Melbourne

Shredded Chicken and Prawns with Vietnamese Slaw and Coriander
Chin Chin

Serves 6–8

500g green prawns, peeled

1 x 1kg whole roast chicken, skin removed and meat shredded

1 fennel bulb, finely sliced

2 red shallots, finely sliced

½ bunch of chive flowers, cut into 2.5cm lengths

¼ savoy cabbage, finely shredded

2 carrots, peeled and shredded

2 celery stalks, finely sliced

100g snow pea tendrils, cut into 2.5cm lengths

1 bunch of Vietnamese mint, leaves picked

1 bunch of coriander, l eaves picked

1 long red chilli, finely sliced

1 Lebanese cucumber, deseeded and cut into half moons

Nuoc nam

200ml lime juice

100ml fish sauce

2–3 teaspoons caster sugar

2 limes, peeled and segmented

4 green bird's eye chillies, finely sliced

2 red bird's eye chillies, finely sliced

Burnt chilli mayonnaise

3 dried long red chillies

100g Kewpie mayonnaise, plus extra for dressing

50ml adjard syrup (equal parts sugar and rice vinegar, brought to the boil and simmered for 5 minutes)

2 tablespoons tamarind water

salt flakes

This Chin Chin staple started as a simple discussion between chef Benjamin Cooper and restaurateur Chris Lucas; the latter wanted a light salad on the menu. Cooper jumped into the kitchen and began experimenting with the ingredients he had on hand. Inspired by summer, the chicken coleslaw with burnt chilli mayo was born.

'It just came together. It is light and summery but still has a bit of balls to it because of the smoky, fieriness of the mayo,' says Cooper. 'And everyone loves mayonnaise. I certainly do.' The burnt chilli mayo makes all the difference – the smoky peppers are pan-fried until blackened, the egg and vinegar curb the heat and the tamarind and adjard syrup (sugar and rice vinegar) round it all out.

Cooper eats the coleslaw three times a week, whether as a healthy lunch option, a pick-me-up in the afternoon, a protein-packed meal after the gym or a light dinner. He describes the salad as a vehicle for other ingredients, encouraging experimentation. 'You could quite as easily throw in some pickled red cabbage or toasted cashews and it works really well with roast meats, like beautiful pork belly or even a poached egg,' he says.

For the nuoc nam, combine all the ingredients in a small bowl – it should be tart and savoury, adjust the balance if necessary.

Add 100ml of the nuoc nam to a medium saucepan with 500ml of water and bring up to a simmer. Add the prawns and poach until just cooked. Drain and set aside.

For the burnt chilli mayonnaise, toast the chillies in a dry frying pan until blackened. Crush coarsely using a mortar and pestle, combine with the remaining ingredients and season with salt to taste.

To make the dressing, combine 150ml of the nuoc nam with 3 tablespoons of the burnt chilli mayonnaise, or to taste.

Combine the prawns with the remaining ingredients in a large bowl and pour over the dressing to taste. Mix with your hands until well combined. Arrange on a large platter and serve. This salad is perfect with cold beer and roti bread.

Leftover burnt chilli mayonnaise will keep for 10–12 days refrigerated in an airtight container, and is great with chicken wings, roast chicken, steak sandwiches, hamburgers and grilled prawns.

CHIN
CHIN

Chin Chin, Melbourne

Chin Chin, Melbourne

234 Clarendon Street
South Melbourne

Pork Bánh Mì
N. Lee Bakery Cafe

Makes 6 rolls

- 6 Vietnamese bánh mì rolls (do not substitute with sourdough or brioche, as it is all about the crunchiness and density of the roll in combination with the fillings)
- 500g chả lụa (Vietnamese pork terrine wrapped in banana leaves, available from Asian grocers), finely sliced
- 2 Lebanese cucumbers, sliced lengthways 2–3mm thick
- 1 bunch of coriander, leaves and fine stems picked
- 3 bird's eye chillies, finely sliced
- ground black pepper
- soy sauce (N. Lee recommends Knorr brand)

Pâté

- 250g fresh chicken livers
- salt flakes
- 65ml canola oil
- 2 teaspoons crushed garlic
- 1 small onion, diced
- 2 teaspoons caster sugar
- 1 tablespoon ground black pepper
- 25g unsalted butter

Pickled carrot and onion

- 625ml white vinegar
- 1 cup plus 2 tablespoons caster sugar
- 2 teaspoons salt flakes
- 2 large carrots, julienned
- 1 small red onion, sliced into 2mm rings

→

Traditional bánh mì is a labour of love. You have to start with the proper foundation, a real bánh mì roll, light and fluffy on the inside, crunchy on the outside, but still dense enough to hold the fillings. N. Lee's roll recipe is top secret; it's prepared at the Smith Street store and then baked on-site, but you can buy yours from any Vietnamese bakery.

Then there are the carrot and onion pickles, which rest in a vinegar solution for at least two hours before serving. And the chicken liver pâté is good enough to eat in isolation. But it's the juicy red pork that is the bánh mì star.

Also known as Vietnamese pork rolls, bánh mì first appeared in Australia in the 1970s, made by the migrants who set up Vietnamese bakeries in the outer suburbs. N. Lee Bakery has been providing Melbourne with bánh mì since the first store opened on Smith Street 25 years ago. This five-part recipe from the N. Lee family is an insight into the consideration that goes into each Vietnamese roll.

This recipe will need to be started the day before serving.

For the pâté, rinse the livers and trim off any sinew. Drain and add to a medium bowl with enough water to cover, add a pinch of salt and stir to dissolve. Cover and refrigerate overnight.

The next day, drain the livers and rinse thoroughly.

In a small saucepan, heat a splash of oil over medium heat. Add the garlic and stir for 10 seconds. Add the onion and cook for 6–7 minutes until softened and translucent. Add the remaining oil and heat for 1 minute. Add the livers, 1 teaspoon of salt, the sugar, pepper and butter and cook over medium heat for 3–4 minutes on one side. Flip and cook until the livers are just cooked through. Cool the mix to room temperature.

Puree the cooled liver mix in a food processor or blender until smooth. Transfer to an airtight container or jar and refrigerate. Pâté can keep for 3–4 days, but it's best consumed the next day.

→

Pork loaf

4 garlic cloves, crushed with the flat of a knife

5 thin slices of ginger

1 teaspoon caster sugar

salt flakes

⅛ teaspoon Chinese red dye (optional, this gives the pork skin colour)

500g pork shoulder, skin on

Mayonnaise

1 egg, separated

1 pinch of salt flakes

125ml canola oil

For the pickles, combine the vinegar, sugar, salt and 500ml of water in a large bowl. Stir until the salt and sugar have dissolved. Add the carrot and onion to separate pickling jars or containers and pour over the liquid to cover. Stir through to make sure there are no air pockets. Cover and refrigerate for 2 hours. The pickles can keep for several weeks but are best consumed the next day or in the first week.

For the pork loaf, place a medium saucepan of water over medium heat and bring to a simmer. Add the garlic, ginger, sugar, 1 teaspoon of salt and the dye, if using.

Meanwhile, clean the pork by rubbing a pinch of salt all over the meat and skin. Rinse under running water.

Place the pork in the pan and poach on medium heat for about 1½ hours until cooked, adding water from time to time to keep the meat submerged. Pierce the pork with a chopstick or skewer and if it goes through the meat smoothly, it's ready. Remove the pork from the liquid and cool to room temperature. Refrigerate, covered, for about 2 hours before using. Slice finely when ready to serve.

For the mayonnaise, add the egg yolk and a third of the egg white to a medium bowl and whisk until pale yellow. Add the salt and continue whisking while slowly drizzling in the oil until incorporated – the mayonnaise should be thick and smooth. Refrigerate in an airtight container until needed.

Cut the rolls in half lengthways and pull open, but ensure the two halves stay attached. Generously spread some pâté on one half and some mayonnaise over the pâté. Arrange slices of chả lụa along the length of the rolls and follow with the pork loaf, cucumber, pickled carrot, pickled onion, coriander and chilli. Grind over some pepper and drizzle with a little soy sauce.

77–79 Nicholson Street
Brunswick East

The Cornish
Pope Joan

Serves 8

- 4 sage leaves
- 120g fresh breadcrumbs
- ½ white onion, diced
- 20g salt flakes, plus extra
- 1 x 1.9kg chicken (Pope Joan uses Milawa free-range chickens)
- 2½ tablespoons olive oil
- freshly ground black pepper
- 100ml liquid from canned jalapeños
- 250g mayonnaise
- 8 soft English-style bread rolls
- cos lettuce leaves, to serve

Take it from Matt Wilkinson, officially the best sandwich maker in the world: you won't find a better sandwich than The Cornish. It's been on the menu at Wilkinson's cafe and restaurant, Pope Joan, since day one. By the time The Australasian Sandwich Association named Wilkinson the world's best sandwich maker in 2011 (he even beat the guy who designs sandwiches for Marks & Spencer in the UK), Pope Joan was firmly established as a Brunswick East favourite.

'The Cornish came about during a conversation in a car, driving to the country, with a journalist called Richard Cornish. It was only after we'd been open for four years that he actually came in and ate it,' says Wilkinson, who points out that the sandwich's name has a double meaning thanks to his British heritage. Cornish (the journalist, not the sandwich) was chatting about a snack he had eaten in Spain: soft bread loaded with pickled peppers, roast chicken and stuffing. Peppers aren't always in season, so Wilkinson substituted jalapeños. He then asked La Madre bakery to custom-bake a soft, white bap roll, sourced free-range chooks from Milawa, added herbs from the garden and now sells around 400 of The Cornishes each week.

Preheat the oven to 225°C fan-forced (245°C conventional).

Combine the sage, breadcrumbs, onion, 20g of salt and 110ml of warm water in a medium bowl and stuff into the cavity of the chicken. Rub the skin with the oil and season. Roast on a wire rack over a baking tray for 24 minutes. Increase the oven temperature to 250°C fan-forced (270°C conventional) and roast for a further 16 minutes.

Take the chicken out of the oven and slice the skin open between the legs and the body. Roast for a further 5 minutes. Set aside to rest and cool.

Once the chicken has cooled, remove the stuffing and pick all the meat from the bones – this should yield no less than 1.2kg of meat. Roughly chop the meat and finely chop the skin and add to a large bowl with the stuffing. Add the jalapeño liquid and mayonnaise, season to taste and combine.

Add about ⅓ of a cup of chicken mix, or more, to each roll, place some lettuce on top and wrap the rolls in foil. Place in a low oven for 5 minutes to warm.

Leftover chicken mix tastes great in a salad or, Wilkinson suggests, as a filling for a jacket potato. It will keep in the fridge for 3–4 days.

118 Elgin Street
Carlton

Reuben Sandwich
Five Points Deli

Serves 4

- 1.8kg Five Points corned beef, or a good-quality alternative
- 8 slices of dark rye bread
- 8 slices of Swiss cheese
- 800g Five Points sauerkraut, or a good-quality alternative

Thousand island dressing (or 1 jar Five Points thousand island dressing)

- 140g quality whole-egg mayonnaise (Five Points recommends Hellmann's)
- 25g tomato ketchup
- 25ml worcestershire sauce
- 3 teaspoons white wine vinegar
- ½ teaspoon tabasco sauce
- 2 teaspoons finely diced brown onion
- ½ teaspoon crushed garlic
- ½ teaspoon salt flakes

Will and Mick Balleau are the brains behind some of Melbourne's favourite restaurants: Chingón, Le Bon Ton (see page 203), Longhorn Saloon and Five Points Deli. Originally from New Mexico, the brothers are sticking to what they know.

'When my brother and I first moved to Melbourne and started conceptualising Chingón and mapping out our future in restaurants, there were a few things we thought would be good, mainly because it was what we missed the most from home. For me, it was the New York deli,' says Will.

Will's love for the hefty Reuben sandwich stems from the stark contrast of flavours, so dissimilar they balance each other out. There's the sharp acidity of the sauerkraut, the tang of the dressing, the juiciness of the meat and the sweetness of rye. 'It's a winning combination that makes this one of the world's best sandwiches,' says Will.

For the thousand island dressing, add all the ingredients to a bowl and whisk to combine. Refrigerate until needed.

Bring a medium saucepan of water to the boil, add the corned beef in its bag, turn down the heat and simmer for 30 minutes. Turn off the heat and remove the bag after 10 minutes.

Spread one side of all of the bread slices generously with the dressing. Slice the corned beef as thinly as possible and split between the sandwiches. While the beef is still hot, place the cheese on top so that it melts slightly, and place a generous amount of sauerkraut on top. Spread the top slices of bread with the dressing and close the sandwich.

The Reuben is always better toasted, so place them in a sandwich press or under the grill. Once nicely toasted, cut the sandwiches in half and serve.

Yong Green Food, Fitzroy

Soy

211 Gertrude Street
Fitzroy

Fish Pie of Ocean Trout, Prawns, Rockling and Sorrel
Builders Arms Hotel

Serves 6

1 packet puff pastry (or enough to cover your chosen dishes)

300g ocean trout fillet, skin removed, cut into 6cm-long pieces

6 green 'U6' prawns, peeled and halved (or 500–600g whole green prawns, peeled)

950g rockling fillet, skin removed, cut into 6cm-long pieces

12 large sorrel leaves, torn

½ cup chopped dill

zest of 1 lemon

3 tablespoons chopped capers

1 egg, beaten

Sauce

3 tablespoons olive oil

3 brown onions, finely sliced

2 garlic cloves, finely sliced

1 large fennel bulb, cored and finely sliced

5 prawn heads

180ml white wine

300g potatoes, peeled and sliced

625ml chicken stock

185ml thickened cream

salt flakes and freshly ground black pepper

When Andrew McConnell first took over the Builders Arms Hotel with business partners Anthony Hammond and head chef Josh Murphy, they asked their friends what they wanted to see on a pub menu. The answer: pie. The Builders Arms Hotel breaks away from the predictable beef option by serving this aromatic fish pie. 'Writing a menu for a pub was something really new to both of us,' says Murphy. 'We were trying to work out how to incorporate a fish dish into the menu, and we'd always toyed with the idea of a fish pie.'

The fish pie was on the first menu when the Builders reopened at the start of autumn 2012. 'We expected to take it off in summer, but we just couldn't; it was too popular,' admits Murphy. 'It's made it through multiple summers now and I don't think we'll ever take it off.' According to one English customer fluent in fish pies, there's a rule of thumb when eating one (with which Murphy concurs): take the lid off, drop the chips in and then scoop them out with a fork to maximise the juices.

For the sauce, heat the oil in a large, heavy-based saucepan and gently cook the onion, garlic and fennel until softened, about 5–6 minutes. Add the prawn heads and cook until pink, about 3–4 minutes. Increase the heat, deglaze the pan with the wine and simmer for 3–4 minutes until almost totally reduced. Add the potatoes and stock and simmer gently until the potatoes are tender and the stock has reduced by two-thirds, about 15–20 minutes. Add the cream, bring the mixture to the boil and turn off the heat. Remove the prawn heads, tip the mix into a blender and puree until smooth. Strain the sauce and season to taste.

Preheat the oven to 190°C fan-forced (210°C conventional).

Cut shapes out of the puff pastry to top the pies with – use one of the pie dishes (500ml ramekins will work well for this) as a template, just be sure to cut the pastry about 1cm wider than the dish all the way around.

Divide the seafood, herbs, lemon zest and capers between the pie dishes. Spoon about 200ml of the sauce into each dish and stir to distribute evenly. Dampen the edges of the bowls with a little water and place the pastry lids on top. Press the pastry lightly onto the dishes and brush with a little beaten egg. Pierce a couple of holes in the top of each pie to let the steam escape and bake for 15–20 minutes until the pastry is golden and the fish is cooked.

enjoy

643–645 Sydney Road
Brunswick

Spinach Triangles
A1 Bakery

Makes 20 triangles

Dough

2 tablespoons honey

1 teaspoon dried yeast

2 tablespoons vegetable oil, plus extra to brush the pastry

900ml warm water

1kg white or wholemeal plain flour

1 teaspoon fine salt

Filling

1kg baby spinach leaves, shredded

2 brown onions, finely diced

125ml lemon juice

3 tablespoons vegetable oil

5 teaspoons ground sumac

2 teaspoons salt flakes

½ teaspoon ground cinnamon

½ teaspoon Lebanese seven spice (baharat)

There's no better example of Melbourne's cultural melting pot than Brunswick's Sydney Road. Nepalese, Indonesian, Malaysian and Greek restaurants sit side-by-side. But ask someone on the street where to find the best value-for-money Lebanese snacks and they're likely to point you in the direction of A1 Bakery. Originally founded by two sisters and their husbands, A1 has been feeding hungry locals since 1992. Traditional pizzas and falafel abound, but for a couple of gold coins the spinach pies are little triangles of ecstasy. The filling can be made in bulk using fresh leaves, onion and lemon juice. Once baked, a zesty sumac and cinnamon aroma comes from the golden pastry making it hard to stop at one. Although best served hot, they also make perfect snacks for school lunchboxes.

To make the dough, combine the honey, yeast, oil and water in a large jug. Add the flour and salt to the bowl of a stand mixer and mix on low speed with the dough hook while gradually adding the liquid, increasing the speed to medium as the mix comes together. If the mix becomes too wet, just add a little more flour. Mix for about 10 minutes until the dough is smooth and relatively soft. Cover with a tea towel and rest for 30–40 minutes.

Once rested, gently turn the dough out onto a floured benchtop. Portion the dough into 100g pieces and roll into balls. Roll each ball in flour and rest on a floured surface somewhere warm, covered, to prove for about 20–30 minutes.

Preheat the oven to 260°C fan-forced (280°C conventional). Line two baking trays with baking paper.

While the dough rests, add all the filling ingredients to a large bowl and mix thoroughly with your hands. Stand for 10 minutes before tipping into a large colander to drain off any excess liquid.

Take a ball of rested dough and roll out into a circle about 22–23cm in diameter. Place a generous handful (about ¾ cup) of the filling in the middle and flatten out into a triangle with the points at 12, 4 and 8 o'clock. Pick up the edges of the dough at 10 o'clock and 2 o'clock and fold over the filling. Pinch the edges together and then fold the 6 o'clock flap over. Pinch the corners and seams together so the parcel doesn't leak and lightly brush with oil. Repeat for the remaining dough and filling. Bake on the prepared trays for about 15 minutes until golden.

Mamasita

11 Collins Street
Melbourne

'I don't think Mexican has even really begun,' says Matt Lane of Mamasita when asked if he thinks Mexican food has had its moment. 'Mexico is one of those places where every region is like a different country. There are many dishes that are very specific to each region. When you're there, you realise we're just at the tip of the iceberg.'

Aguachile (cured trout, see page 111) and Cochinita Pibil (pork hock, see page 109) are two such regional dishes. The first comes from Sinaloa, just north of Mexico City on the Pacific Coast; the latter is a Yucatan dish from down south.

'The difference between aguachile and ceviche is that ceviche is marinated for up to 5 or 6 hours before serving. We cure the aguachile with lime to order – it's almost cruda, almost raw,' explains co-owner and restaurant manager, Nick Peters. Usually served in Mexico on Saltines (like Salada crackers), Mamasita uses fish skin crisped in the oven. 'Whenever I make a fish dish at home I buy it with skin on so that I can save it to make chicharrónes (traditionally made with pork rind, but in this case fried fish skins), because they keep.'

The pibil is more of a celebratory dish. Pibil is a Mayan word that means 'buried' and it's traditionally wrapped in banana leaf and cooked in a pit fire. The achiote spice paste contains annatto seed, which gives the pork its colour, while the addition of citrus and the sourness from the pickled onions balances it all out when served with fresh corn tortillas, guacamole and rice.

11 Collins Street
Melbourne

Cochinita Pibil (Slow-Roasted Achiote Pork, Pineapple and Onion Escabeche)
Mamasita

Serves 4–6

1 pineapple

1 x 1.2kg fresh pork hock

150ml orange juice

500g banana leaves (available fresh or frozen at Asian grocers)

fresh corn tortillas, to serve

guacamole, to serve

rice, to serve

Marinade

20 garlic cloves

½ cinnamon stick, dry roasted and ground

150g achiote paste

1 teaspoon cumin seeds, roasted and ground

3 cloves, roasted and ground

15g chilli flakes

1 teaspoon dried oregano

1 teaspoon salt flakes

150ml orange juice

Pickled onions

125ml white wine vinegar

75g caster sugar

1 red onion, halved and cut into 1cm slices

The pickled onions need to be made a day before serving.

For the pickled onions, bring the vinegar to a simmer in a medium saucepan and stir in the sugar until dissolved. Add the onion to a medium bowl and pour over the pickling liquid. Refrigerate for 24 hours.

Preheat the oven to 180°C fan-forced (200°C conventional).

Place the whole pineapple on a baking tray and roast for 40 minutes. Cool in the refrigerator, and then peel with a knife and split into quarters. Remove and discard the core, slice into 4cm chunks and set aside.

For the marinade, add all the ingredients except the orange juice to a food processor and blend until smooth. Tip into a medium bowl and stir in the juice.

Add the pork to a large bowl and rub with 100g of the marinade. Marinate in the refrigerator for at least 3 hours.

Preheat the oven to 160°C fan-forced (180°C conventional). Line an ovenproof dish with the banana leaves, leaving enough leaves overhanging the dish to fold over the top of the pork.

Remove the pork from the fridge, add the orange juice and mix well with the marinade in the bowl. Place the pork in the prepared dish and pour all the marinade from the bowl over the top. Fold the leaves over to encase the pork. Cover tightly with foil and bake for about 3 hours until the pork is tender to the touch. Remove from the oven and cool for 20 minutes, covered.

Remove the pork from the dish, reserving all the cooking liquor. Tear the meat into chunky pieces using two forks – you can discard the skin now if you like, but Mamasita insists it's the best bit. Pour the reserved cooking juices over the meat and mix well to coat all the meat evenly.

Transfer the pork to a serving dish, scatter over the pickled onions and pineapple and serve with fresh corn tortillas, guacamole and rice.

Leftover marinade will keep for up to 1 month refrigerated, or can be frozen, and is great for barbecued chicken and prawns as well as with other cuts of pork.

11 Collins Street
Melbourne

Aguachile (Ocean Trout Crudo with Habanero, Jicama, Lime Granita and Fish Chicharrón)
Mamasita

Serves 4

250g ocean trout fillet, pin-boned, skin removed and reserved to make the chicharrón

salt flakes

1 litre vegetable oil

1 Lebanese cucumber, seeds discarded, cut into 1cm dice

1 jicama (or small daikon), peeled and cut into 1cm dice

½ red onion, very finely sliced

Lime granita

25g caster sugar

25ml lime juice

2 teaspoons olive oil

Habanero vinaigrette

3 teaspoons habanero hot sauce (Mamasita makes their own, but use your favourite)

25ml apple cider vinegar

125ml blended oil

Remove any excess fat and flesh from the fish skin with a blunt knife or the edge of a teaspoon. Lightly salt the skin and place in the fridge for several hours to cure and dry.

Meanwhile, to make the granita, bring 75ml of water to a simmer in a small saucepan and whisk in the sugar until dissolved. Remove from the heat and cool to room temperature. Combine the lime juice and oil with the cooled syrup, pour into a wide, shallow dish (preferably stainless steel to speed up the freezing process) and place in the freezer for 1 hour. After the first 30 minutes, use a fork to scrape the forming ice to break apart the crystals. Place back in the freezer. Repeat this process every 10 minutes until the finished granita looks like powdery snow – how long this takes will depend on the thickness of the ice due to the size of the dish.

Preheat the oven to 90°C fan-forced (110°C conventional).

Remove the fish skin from the fridge and place on a baking tray. Place the tray in the oven for 3 hours to completely dry out the skin. Once cooled, the skin will be quite crisp and brittle.

Heat the vegetable oil in a medium saucepan to 180°C.

Tear the skin into 2.5–3cm pieces. Carefully drop one piece into the oil to test the temperature. If it doesn't puff up like a prawn cracker, the oil isn't hot enough. Once up to temperature, cook the skin for 30 seconds and drain on paper towel.

For the habanero vinaigrette, combine the hot sauce with the vinegar in a small bowl. Slowly add the oil while whisking. Once combined, refrigerate in an airtight container until required.

Using a sharp knife, slice the fish on a 45-degree angle into 3mm-thick sheets and lay flat on a serving plate. Lightly season the fish with salt, scatter generously with the cucumber, jicama and onion and dress with the habanero vinaigrette to taste. Top with some lime granita, scatter over the chicharrón and serve immediately.

1 Hosier Lane
Melbourne

Pulpo a la Gallega (Galician Octopus)
MoVida

Serves 4–6

1kg frozen large octopus tentacles (about 3 tentacles), thawed and drained

1kg waxy potatoes (such as kipfler), skin on

salt flakes

extra-virgin olive oil, to serve

Spanish sweet paprika, to serve

2 tablespoons very finely chopped flat-leaf parsley

Forget everything you've been told about using seafood caught that morning – MoVida swears by using frozen octopus in this signature dish. That's not to say the tentacles aren't fresh, but rather frozen upon arrival, from Fremantle, WA. Chef and co-owner Frank Camorra discovered that the freezing process breaks apart the cell walls of the flesh, causing the meat to tenderise before cooking even begins.

'It's a simple peasant dish that's a lot easier to prepare than, say, calamari. You don't have to clean it or gut it, you just buy the tentacles as they are,' explains kitchen operations manager Steve Rogers. The cooking method, which requires blanching the tentacles five times in boiling water before simmering them, sets the proteins so the pink skin and textural suckers don't disintegrate.

The aim is to find the best produce possible, says Rogers, and then share it in a fun and informal environment. Those who have eaten at the original MoVida on Hosier Lane will know what he's talking about. Solo diners command the bar seats, enjoying a friendly and informative chat about food and wine. Duos and groups revel in the buzz at nearby tables and consider trips to the land of tapas – MoVida's Galician octopus tends to have that effect.

To cook the octopus, bring a large saucepan of unsalted water to a rapid boil.

Meanwhile, wash the octopus under cold running water.

Plunge the octopus into the boiling water for 15 seconds and remove. Allow the water to come to the boil again and repeat the blanching process four times, allowing the water to reach boiling point between each immersion. On the last immersion, leave the octopus in the pan and reduce the heat until barely simmering. Cook for 30–40 minutes until tender. The outside pink layer should still be intact. Remove the octopus from the pan and set aside to cool.

Bring the cooking water back to the boil, then add the potatoes and cook for 20–30 minutes until tender. Drain and set aside until cool enough to handle.

Slice the octopus. Peel the potatoes and slice into 2cm discs.

To serve, place the potato discs on a serving plate and cover with the octopus. Sprinkle with salt, drizzle with a little oil, sprinkle over some paprika and parsley and serve immediately.

45 Collins Street
Melbourne

Tuna, Salted Watermelon and Sriracha Tartare
Pei Modern

Serves 6

3 large sebago or Dutch cream potatoes, skin on

1 litre grapeseed or canola oil

1 teaspoon salt flakes, plus extra (Pei Modern uses Murray River)

500g trimmed seedless watermelon

500g sashimi-grade yellowfin tuna

1 small red onion, very finely diced

1 tablespoon white soy sauce (Japanese light soy sauce)

2 teaspoons sriracha (Pei Modern uses Huy Fong brand)

6 eggs

1 teaspoon sansho pepper

'Good cooking is about the accumulation of all the tiny details,' says Pei Modern's Mark Best (also of Marque in Sydney). For Best, a produce-driven menu isn't a selling point; it's the only way to cook. 'It's about amplifying the inherent qualities of very good produce. That's what Pei is about and it's the same with Marque, that's the common theme between them,' he says.

Best has taken a ubiquitous dish, tuna tartare, and turned it into something more unusual. According to Best, steak tartare often features tabasco sauce, but Best's tuna incorporates sriracha; both are fermented products that bring an umami element to the dishes. 'There are also similarities between the salted watermelon and the meat, and bringing that freshness is what Australian cuisine is all about,' he says.

The secret to the tartare is a sharp knife, but Best warns that those with less kitchen experience shouldn't get ahead of themselves. 'Where home cooks often go wrong is not following the detail of the recipe. They say "a recipe is only a guide" and think the details are arbitrary, but the recipe is only a guide for people who know what they're doing.'

Preheat the oven to 90°C fan-forced (110°C conventional).

Place the potatoes on a baking tray and place in the oven for 1 hour to set the starch. Refrigerate until cool.

Preheat the oil in a medium saucepan to 170°C.

Peel the cooled potatoes and cut into 1mm-thick slices (this is easiest using a mandoline. Pat dry and fry until golden. Season with salt while still hot.

Remove any pith from the watermelon and cut into 1cm-thick slices. Sprinkle with 1 teaspoon of salt and set aside to macerate for 30 minutes.

Trim the tuna of any sinew and cut into 5mm dice. Pat the watermelon dry with paper towel and cut into fine dice.

Add the tuna, watermelon, onion, soy and sriracha to a medium bowl and gently combine. Divide the mix between serving plates and make an indentation in each portion. Separate the eggs and place a yolk in each indentation. Serve with a pile of chips on the side, sprinkled with sansho pepper.

161 Spring Street
Melbourne

Tuna Niçoise
The European

Serves 6

6 small kipfler potatoes, skin on

30–40 green beans

6 eggs

3 tablespoons lemon juice

120ml olive oil, plus extra

1 head of curly endive, inner leaves only

1 small bunch of basil, leaves picked

30 cherry, medley or small heirloom tomatoes, halved

30–40 mixed olives, pitted and cut in half

2 tablespoons blanched peas

6 zucchini flowers, baby zucchini chopped into fine rounds and leaves torn

salt flakes and freshly ground black pepper

12 white anchovy fillets

6 tuna steaks (180–200g each and cut from the loin)

bottarga, to serve

'Ours is more refined [than others],' says head chef Tim Martin of The European's niçoise salad. Originating in Provence, the dish has become a staple in French brasseries and now also at The European. While it traditionally includes canned tuna, boiled eggs, tomatoes, potatoes, lettuce, olives and anchovies, The European's version steps it up with alterations and additions: fresh tuna cooked medium–rare, heirloom tomatoes, white anchovies, zucchini flowers and bottarga (cured fish roe, available at boutique seafood stores). 'We call it a composed salad,' says Martin. 'This means that once all the ingredients are prepared, the salad is assembled piece-by-piece. 'It shows off all the beautiful spring green vegetables.' The dish is served at room temperature, perfect for those who want to prepare everything in advance, aside from the tuna, which should be seared at the last minute.

Add the potatoes to a medium saucepan, cover with cold salted water and bring to the boil. Reduce to a simmer and cook until tender, about 15 minutes. Drain, set aside to cool and then peel and slice into discs.

Bring a medium saucepan of salted water to the boil. Fill a large bowl with ice and water to refresh the beans and eggs.

Blanch the beans until they just change colour, about 1–2 minutes. Lift from the water and refresh in the iced water. Drain and set aside.

Bring the water back to the boil again and gently lower the eggs in with a spoon. Cook for exactly 6 minutes. Refresh in the iced water and peel once completely cool.

Combine the lemon juice and olive oil in a small bowl to make a simple dressing.

Preheat the barbecue on high or a griddle pan over high heat.

Add the endive to a large bowl with the basil, tomatoes, potato, olives, peas, zucchini and zucchini flowers. Dress to taste, season and divide between serving plates.

Tear each egg into three or so pieces and arrange over each salad. Top with the anchovy fillets.

Oil and season the tuna steaks to taste, then grill for 1–2 minutes on each side until cooked to your liking. Place the steaks next to the salads, grate some bottarga over the top and serve.

180 Flinders Lane
Melbourne

New England Lobster Roll
Supernormal

Serves 8

2 lobster tails (about 250g each once shelled)

½ cup Kewpie mayonnaise

2 teaspoons lemon juice

1 teaspoon white wine vinegar

1 teaspoon mustard powder

2 French shallots, cut in half lengthways and finely sliced

8 brioche buns, cut in half horizontally

1 cup picked watercress

3 tablespoons olive oil

salt flakes

butter

The lobster roll at Supernormal has achieved cult status, up there with 400 Gradi's margherita pizza (see page 173) and Lune's croissants (see page 31). They first popped up at Golden Fields in St Kilda after Andrew McConnell sampled something similar on a 2010 trip to New York. Now the lobster roll has made its way to Supernormal, his poppy Asian eatery in Flinders Lane. The menu here is McConnell's interpretation of Asia in Melbourne, a nod to his years spent working in Shanghai and Hong Kong. As for the lobster roll, the meat is from different regions depending on the season, but the soft, sugary rolls are made at Bread Top in Chinatown. McConnell heats them, butters them up and adds sweet Kewpie mayo, available from any Asian grocer. He puts their popularity down to the rolls being, 'A little bit of luxury without having to over-commit.'

Bring a large saucepan of water to the boil and reduce to a simmer over medium heat. Poach the lobster tails in their shells for 15–20 minutes until cooked – a probe thermometer is useful here, with the ideal internal temperature being 63°C. Remove the lobster tails from the pan and set aside to cool, then refrigerate until chilled.

Preheat the oven to 180°C fan-forced (200°C conventional).

Remove the lobster meat from the shells and slice into eight discs per tail. Finely chop any small or discoloured pieces of lobster you may have leftover.

Combine the mayonnaise, lemon juice, vinegar and mustard powder in a small bowl. Slowly add the oil while whisking continually. Season to taste.

Butter the brioche buns lightly. Place them, buttered side down, in an ovenproof frying pan and toast in the oven for about 5 minutes until golden brown.

Spread 1 teaspoon of the mayonnaise on each buttered half of the brioche buns. Place 1 tablespoon of the chopped lobster on the bottom bun and season to taste. Arrange two slices of lobster meat on top without overlapping. Add ½ teaspoon of mayonnaise to each lobster slice and season again to taste. Add a few slices of shallot and a few pieces of watercress, close with the top buns and serve immediately.

Supernormal, Melbourne

Supernormal, Melbourne

14–16 Market Lane
Melbourne

Xiao Long Bao (Soup Dumplings)
HuTong Dumpling Bar

Makes 15 dumplings

100g plain flour

2½ tablespoons cold water

black vinegar, to serve

finely sliced ginger, to serve

Filling

100g minced pork leg

½ teaspoon finely chopped spring onion

½ teaspoon grated ginger

½ teaspoon soy sauce

½ teaspoon oyster sauce

½ teaspoon MSG powder

½ teaspoon chicken powder

½ teaspoon caster sugar

1 pinch of ground black pepper

1 drop of sesame oil

2 tablespoons pork bone soup or stock

These addictive parcels filled with pork and broth have been drawing crowds since HuTong Group opened its first dumpling bar in 2008 down Market Lane in the CBD, and soon after in Prahran at the Cullen Hotel. Back at the original, kids press their faces against the glass window that looks through to the kitchen, and diners watch as dumpling masters assemble each tiny package with the flick of a wrist.

HuTong Prahran head chef, Jun Jing Hua, has been making xiao long bao for more than a decade, so there's no need to worry if you don't perfect them right away. The chef has a few tips that are invaluable for first-timers: lightly flour the bench before rolling your dough to avoid having to scrape it off later; always make it fresh (it's easier to secure it around the filling this way); and make sure there are no holes in the wrapping. To make the soup, the HuTong kitchen boils pork skin until it turns to jelly before mixing it with the filling. At home, your best bet is to use chicken or pork bone stock. If you have the time, homemade is always best.

Place the flour on a wooden pastry board, add the cold water in two or three additions and knead until a dough forms. Wrap in plastic wrap and set aside on the bench for 20 minutes.

Add all the filling ingredients apart from the stock to a blender along with 1 teaspoon of water and blend until smooth. Blend in the stock and refrigerate, covered, until needed.

Roll the dough into a long rope on a floured benchtop and cut into 15 pieces of about 10g each. Using a rolling pin, roll each piece into a circle about 10cm in diameter, with the skin thicker in the middle and quite thin at the edges. Portion the meat mixture and place in the middle of each skin. Bring up the sides and pinch to close the dumplings, ensuring that the dumplings are sealed and that there are no holes in the skins.

Add the dumplings to a bamboo steamer lined with baking paper (with holes poked in the paper to allow the steam to circulate) and steam for about 8–10 minutes over a saucepan of boiling water. Do not overcook as the skins may split.

Once cooked, serve immediately with the black vinegar and finely sliced ginger.

421 Brunswick Street
Fitzroy

Charcoal Noodle and Pine Nut Soup with Fried Kombu
Yong Green Food

Serves 4

½ cup soybeans, soaked overnight in water and drained

½ cup pine nuts

1 teaspoon salt flakes

360g dried charcoal noodles (or your favourite noodles)

125ml coconut oil

4 x 5cm pieces of kombu (edible kelp)

4 spring onions, root ends only, cut into 1cm lengths (so they look like little paintbrushes)

1 teaspoon coconut sugar (or to taste)

4 small king brown mushrooms, quartered lengthways

1 Lebanese cucumber, julienned

12 cherry tomatoes, halved

kimchi, to serve

Batter

1 tablespoon rice flour

2 teaspoons potato starch

2 tablespoons soy milk

1 pinch of cayenne pepper

salt flakes

Yong Green Food is owned by two Korean sisters, Seon Mi and Seon Joo Lee. Their philosophy is to tread lightly upon nature by serving wholesome vegetarian food. This dish calls for charcoal noodles, available at Asian grocers, but you can also use rice or gluten-free soba noodles. Once prepared, they swim in a shallow soybean and pine nut soup with fried kombu, cucumber, tomato and spring onion. Adding a sprinkle of coconut sugar and serving the noodles with kimchi results in an exciting combination of sweet and savoury with a touch of spice.

Place the soybeans in a large saucepan and cover well with water. Bring up to the boil, reduce to a simmer and cook for 2½–3 hours until tender. To speed this process up, soak the soybeans in boiling water for 1 hour, drain and cook in a pressure cooker for 20–25 minutes until tender. Drain the cooked soybeans and rinse.

Add the soybeans, pine nuts, salt and 500ml of water to a blender or food processor and blend until smooth. Keep the soup warm in a medium saucepan on the stovetop.

Cook the noodles according to the packet instructions.

To make the batter, add all the ingredients to a bowl, season and beat until combined.

Heat the coconut oil in a frying pan over high heat. Fry the kombu and spring onion roots until golden brown. Drain on paper towel and toss with the coconut sugar.

Lightly coat the mushrooms with the batter and fry until golden.

Arrange the noodles in serving bowls and pour over the hot soup. Top with the cucumber, tomatoes, kombu, spring onion roots and mushrooms and serve with the kimchi on the side.

264 Victoria Street
Richmond

Thit Kho Taù (Braised Pork Belly and Egg Claypot)

I Love Phở

Serves 4

1kg pork belly (not too fatty), cut into large cubes

vegetable oil, for frying

½ brown onion, finely sliced

750ml coconut water

8 hard-boiled eggs

fine coriander sprigs, to serve

sliced cucumber, to serve

carrot and radish pickles, to serve

steamed rice, to serve

Marinade

2 garlic cloves, finely chopped

4 red shallots, finely chopped

2 spring onions, finely chopped

3 tablespoons fish sauce

2 tablespoons grated palm sugar

salt and ground black pepper

It's a long-standing debate in Melbourne: which restaurant on Victoria Street – Melbourne's iconic Vietnamese strip in Richmond – does the best phở. I Love Phở has been a consistent standout. But rather than hand over its principal dish, the family behind the specialty shop chose to share a traditional favourite. 'It's something we've eaten since we were kids,' says Hung Vo, the son of I Love Phở's founders Hien and Tan Vo. 'It's a quick, simple and tasty meal that grandma and mum like to cook all the time because it's so convenient. I eat it at least once a week.' Vo says it's often served as part of a banquet at gatherings, making it the ideal meal for entertaining. Those who don't eat pork belly can replace it with fish.

You will need a claypot for this recipe.

Add all the marinade ingredients to a large bowl, season and stir until the sugar has dissolved. Add the pork, mix well, cover and marinate in the fridge for a minimum of 20 minutes, ideally an hour.

Heat 3 teaspoons of oil in a large frying pan over medium–high heat. Add the onion and fry until fragrant. Add the pork and cook until evenly coloured, about 4–5 minutes. Add the contents of the pan to a claypot with any residual marinade. Add the coconut water and 500ml of water and bring to the boil. Turn the heat down to low and simmer for 1 hour, skimming any impurities as they appear. Meanwhile, fry the eggs over high heat until golden, about 1–2 minutes.

Once the pork is cooked, finish with some coriander and serve in the pot with the eggs, cucumber, pickled carrot and radish, and rice on the side.

106 Smith Street
Collingwood

Huxtaburger
Huxtaburger

Serves 4

400g wagyu beef mince

salt flakes and freshly ground black pepper

2 teaspoons vegetable oil

4 slices of cheddar cheese

4 soft buns (from an Asian bakery), sliced open

clarified butter, to brush the buns

tomato ketchup

pickles

mustard

4 slices of tomato

4 iceberg lettuce leaves, torn

½ cup mayonnaise

Not long after chef Daniel Wilson and his business partners brought us Huxtable in 2010, they began to sell burgers across the road at Huxtaburger that soon had people queuing. Wilson has a few key tips for perfecting something seemingly simple:

1. Always use quality ingredients and don't be shy with condiments.
2. The bun's role is to hold the patty in place, so make sure it's the same circumference as the bun. 'It should not be a rissole in a loaf of bread!'
3. Brushing the inside of the bun with melted butter or olive oil before toasting it on a flat grill or pan not only makes the inside crisp, but also softens the bun by steaming it a little.
4. The pan or grill has to be hot enough for the meat to caramelise.
5. 'Much like life, balance is the key in a burger. The burger should be a sum of all of its parts and they should all be there for a reason. There are no rules, but if it seems weird, it probably is.'

Preheat the flat grill of the barbecue on high, or a large heavy-based frying pan over high heat.

Add the mince to a medium bowl, season and mix with your hands. Divide into 100g portions and form into patties the size of your buns.

Add the oil to the grill or pan and cook the patties until brown, about 1–2 minutes. Flip and place the cheese on top of each patty and cook for another 1–2 minutes, or until cooked to your liking.

Meanwhile, brush the buns with the clarified butter and toast them on the flat grill.

Add some ketchup to the bottom buns followed by some pickles, the patties, mustard, tomato and lettuce. Spread some mayonnaise on the top bun, close the burger and serve.

Rear 412 Brunswick Street
Fitzroy

Sichuan Lamb Spare Ribs, Pickled Dill Cucumber and Nashi Salad

Hammer & Tong 412

'Everyone loves meat on a rib these days,' says chef Simon Ward, co-owner of Hammer & Tong 412. Its Sichuan version is a seriously popular dish, often served at special events. 'The ribs are really, really tender but crispy on the outside and the Sichuan spice mix that we use infuses the meat.'

Ward and his business partner Dennis Ferreira are both ex-Vue de Monde and the former fills the menu with everything from savoury marshmallows and mousses to jellies and gels. But it was head chef of the daytime team, Emma Jeffrey, who came up with the idea for this recipe, which according to Ward, 'Just went off.' The pickled dill and fennel pollen vinaigrette packs a zingy punch, while the freshness of the nashi, cucumber and mint cuts through the oiliness of the meat. These flavour combinations make it easy to keep going back for more.

Because most domestic ovens don't have a 'steam' option, Ward suggests, 'Making a basic bain-marie and putting tin foil over it so the steam penetrates the meat, as opposed to directly grilling it or putting it straight into the oven. That way it stays really tender.' Try pairing the ribs with a dry riesling – the tannins in heavy reds enhance spice while a sweet white will balance it out.

Serves 4–6

1 x 1kg rack lamb spare ribs

2 Lebanese cucumbers

oil, for deep-frying

1 nashi pear

10 mint leaves

½ teaspoon black sesame seeds

lime cheeks, to serve

Marinade

3 teaspoons Sichuan peppercorns

1 teaspoon coriander seeds

1 teaspoon fennel seeds

1 teaspoon cumin seeds

1 teaspoon smoked paprika

1 teaspoon chilli flakes

100ml peanut oil

2 tablespoons light soy sauce

2 tablespoons grated palm sugar

2 tablespoons rice wine vinegar

Lamb seasoning

3 tablespoons Sichuan peppercorns

1 tablespoon coriander seeds

2 tablespoons salt flakes

1 tablespoon chilli powder

2 teaspoons ground ginger

2 teaspoons onion powder

2 teaspoons garlic powder

1 tablespoon smoked paprika

2 tablespoons caster sugar

→

Cut the ribs so that they fit into a large steamer and steam over a saucepan of simmering water for 60–80 minutes until tender, topping up the water as necessary – the slower and longer you cook the ribs the better the result. Cool slightly, then cut into individual or double ribs.

Meanwhile, for the marinade, coarsely grind the whole spices using either a mortar and pestle or spice grinder. Add the ground spices, paprika, chilli flakes and liquid ingredients to a large bowl and combine. Add the ribs and rub the marinade all over. Set aside for 1 hour.

For the lamb seasoning, toast the Sichuan peppercorns and coriander seeds in a dry frying pan over medium heat until fragrant – this process brings the natural oils out in the seeds and yields a better end result. Add the remaining ingredients, except the sugar, and heat for another 2–3 minutes. Cool the spices, add the sugar and grind to a very fine powder.

→

Dill pollen dressing

200ml white balsamic vinegar

150g caster sugar

1 pinch of dill pollen (or dried dill if you can't find dill pollen)

zest of 2 limes

To make the dill pollen dressing, add the white balsamic and sugar to a small saucepan and reduce by a quarter over medium heat. Chill before adding the dill pollen and lime zest.

To prepare the cucumber, adjust a mandoline blade to about a 3mm setting with the julienne cutter attached. Slice each cucumber lengthways into long spaghetti strips, rotating a quarter turn once you reach the soft core. Repeat until all that is left is core. Discard the core, add the strips to a medium bowl and set aside.

Preheat a deep-fryer to 180°C.

Deep-fry the ribs until the outside is crisp, about 2–3 minutes. Don't fry for too long, as the ribs are already cooked and you want to keep them moist. Add to a large bowl and generously sprinkle over the lamb seasoning, coating the ribs all over.

Slice the nashi finely and remove the core. Add to the cucumber spaghetti and dress with enough dill pollen dressing to coat lightly. Add the mint and sesame seeds and toss through.

Plate the ribs with the cucumber and nashi salad and lime cheeks on the side.

288 Smith Street
Collingwood

Home-Style Fried Chicken
Rockwell and Sons

Serves 2–4

1 x 1.1kg chicken (the best you can afford)

100g salt

8 thyme sprigs

1 x 15cm rosemary sprig

4 parsley stalks

2 fresh bay leaves

1 small onion, sliced

6 garlic cloves, smashed

zest of 1 lemon

1 tablespoon black peppercorns

1½ teaspoons chilli flakes

500g ice

500ml buttermilk

2 tablespoons hot sauce

peanut or cottonseed oil, for deep-frying

Seasoned flour

1½ cups plain flour

3 teaspoons cornflour

3 teaspoons baking powder

1 tablespoon fine salt

1 tablespoon ground black pepper

1 tablespoon paprika

1 tablespoon chilli powder

'If there's a picnic, you bring fried chicken; if there's a graduation you have fried chicken; if there's a death in the family people drop it off so you don't have to cook – it's the cornerstone of Southern food.'

That's Casey Wall, co-owner of Rockwell and Sons. Originally from North Carolina, the American chef started the first draft of his recipe when one of the owners of Le Cirque, the French institution where he was working, asked him to cook up some fried chicken to eat during a football game.

'It blew up,' says Wall. 'It just went nuts and then I had to make it all the time.' Wall and his chicken recipe landed in Collingwood in 2012, after a stint working at Cutler & Co., when Rockwell and Sons opened. His timing couldn't have been better. 'The GFC was responsible for fried chicken. There were a lot of Australians going to the States at that time, and that's what sparked the American craze,' says Wall. This recipe, modified for the home cook, takes a few hours instead of the usual four days.

Wall suggests using a neutral cooking oil, ideally peanut, but cottonseed is second best if you have an allergy. Because chicken contains a lot of moisture, using a pot for this recipe is more likely to result in it getting burnt. Stick to a domestic deep-fryer set to 175°C and fill according to the manufacturer's instructions.

You will need a benchtop deep-fryer and a probe thermometer for this recipe.

Cut the chicken into eight pieces (keep the backbone and wingtips for stock or gravy).

Add the salt, herbs, onion, garlic, lemon zest, peppercorns, chilli flakes and 500ml of water to a medium saucepan and bring to the boil. Turn off the heat and stand for 10 minutes.

Pour the brine into a large container, add the ice and stand until the ice has melted. Strain and pour the liquid over the chicken in a bowl or container that fits everything quite snugly. This is a 10% brine and will brine the chicken in a fairly express manner; Rockwell and Sons does it for a day at a much lower salinity, but this version works well and it's a lot quicker. As long as you keep the salinity levels correct, you can add whatever flavouring aromatics you like. Refrigerate for 2 hours.

→

Drain the brined chicken in a colander and stand for 30 minutes before adding to a large container.

Combine the buttermilk and hot sauce and pour over the chicken. Marinate for 30 minutes.

Preheat a deep-fryer to 175°C.

For the seasoned flour, combine all the ingredients in a large bowl.

Remove the chicken from the buttermilk. The buttermilk will be used to dredge the chicken and needs to be the consistency of thin yoghurt, so whisk through a little of the seasoned flour if necessary.

When ready to cook – make sure to do this just before cooking – dredge the chicken in the seasoned flour, then the buttermilk and back in the seasoned flour. Place on a wire rack while you dredge the remaining chicken. Fry the chicken for about 8 minutes until the internal temperature reaches 75°C. Rest for 2 minutes on a wire rack before serving.

400 Gradi, Brunswick East

Dinner

→

Izakaya Den, Melbourne

150–156 Gertrude Street
Fitzroy

Drinks before Dinner
with Michael Madrusan of The Everleigh

Kick the evening off with a little fanfare when making cocktails at home. Whether it's a nice ritual at the end of a day, or a special treat when having friends over, much like following a recipe for food, you can enjoy the process of making cocktails as well as drinking them.

They don't have to be too fancy, but a little know-how can go a long way. Here, Michael Madrusan of The Everleigh, Heartbreaker and Navy Strength Ice Co. shares some of his go-to aperitifs. The key to sophisticated cocktails lies in the ingredients. 'Be sure to use good-quality spirits and fresh ingredients,' says Madrusan. 'These are simple drinks. They rely on the strengths of each individual component. If one is of poor quality, it will throw out the balance in the drink.'

All fresh, light and sometimes bitter, these drinks help whet the palate for the meal to come without assaulting the tastebuds and filling the stomach.

A few tips:

Chill your glassware. It will keep your drinks cool longer and enhance the experience.

Make garnishes using a Y or potato peeler, but don't peel too close to the pith, as it will add bitterness to your drink. And be careful with your fingers when peeling.

To make a basic sugar syrup, mix equal parts caster sugar to hot water, measuring both by weight for accuracy. Stir together until the liquid is clear. Keep in the fridge for up to 1 week.

Sherry Lady

Serves 1

25ml fresh fino sherry

25ml gin

25ml freshly squeezed lemon juice

25ml Cointreau

5ml sugar syrup (see recipe above)

ice

1 lemon, to serve

Here you have an especially light and wonderfully refreshing, dryer-style drink. The Sherry Lady is based on the Sidecar cocktail, a well-known classic originating in 1920s Europe. Enjoy a round of these before the wine is served at a dinner party.

Add all of the ingredients to a cocktail shaker filled with ice and shake hard to chill and mix completely. A quick, hard shake helps create a lighter-style drink and gives life to these ingredients.

Using a cocktail strainer, strain your drink into a chilled champagne saucer or cocktail glass.

Finally, garnish with a twist of lemon.

→

French 125

Serves 1

30ml cognac

15ml freshly squeezed lemon juice

15ml sugar syrup (see recipe on page 143)

About 60ml cold champagne or sparkling wine (the amount will vary depending on the size of your glass)

1 lemon, to serve

The French 125 and the French 75 (which swaps cognac for gin) are both classic cocktails that mix champagne and liquor with fresh citrus. They're short, light and refreshing and best enjoyed before a celebratory meal or alongside light fare at a social gathering.

Add the cognac, lemon juice and sugar syrup to a shaker filled with ice. Shake briefly. This will ensure the ingredients are well combined without becoming too watery.

Using a cocktail strainer, strain the liquid into a chilled champagne saucer or cocktail glass.

Top up the glass with cold champagne or sparkling wine and garnish with a twist of lemon.

American Negroni

Serves 1

10ml Aperol

10ml Campari

20ml fresh sweet vermouth

60ml bourbon

dash of Angostura bitters

ice

1 orange, to serve

This drink is a great twist on a classic Boulevardier cocktail, which was invented in Paris around 1927. The American Negroni evokes qualities of both the Boulevardier and the ever-popular Negroni, with the sweet addition of Aperol – another delicious aperitif. Take note that sweet vermouth has a shelf life of 1 month if kept in the fridge. It's always best to use fresh whenever possible.

Add all of your ingredients to a rocks glass or tumbler filled with ice. Give the drink a gentle stir to mix and slightly chill all of the ingredients.

Garnish with an orange twist.

Cynarita

Serves 1

15ml Cynar

15ml Campari

45ml good-quality blanco tequila

ice

1 lemon, to serve

This drink is a perfect, pre-dinner sipper. The earthiness of the tequila and the bite of Campari – combined with Cynar, which is made from artichoke – results in a beautifully balanced, savoury-style beverage.

Add all of your ingredients to a rocks glass or tumbler filled with ice. Give the drink a gentle stir to mix and slightly chill all of the ingredients.

Garnish with a twist of lemon.

Tom Collins

Serves 1

60ml gin

25ml freshly squeezed lemon juice

25ml sugar syrup (see recipe on page 143)

ice

about 60ml cold soda water (the amount will vary depending on your glass)

slice of orange, to serve

fresh cherry, to serve

This is a light and refreshing drink that's perfect as a palate cleanser before dinner. For a slightly spicier variation, add a few dashes of absinthe for a Dr Fink.

Add the gin, lemon juice and sugar syrup to a shaker filled with ice and shake briefly. This will mix and chill the ingredients without diluting them too much.

Using a cocktail strainer, strain your ingredients into a chilled highball glass filled with ice.

Top up the drink with cold soda water and garnish with a slice of orange and a cherry.

TONKA

20 Duckboard Place
Melbourne

Paneer Zucchini Flowers
Tonka

Serves 6 (3 flowers per serve)

- vegetable oil, for deep-frying
- 18 zucchini flowers
- ⅔ cup glutinous rice flour
- ⅔ cup rice flour
- ⅔ cup tapioca starch
- 180ml cold soda water

Paneer

- 2 litres buffalo milk (not UHT)
- salt flakes
- 2 teaspoons lemon juice

Spice mix

- 2 teaspoons fennel seeds
- 1 teaspoon black peppercorns
- 30g kashmiri chillies

Stuffing

- 1 teaspoon vegetable oil
- 3 fresh curry leaves
- 1 kashmiri chilli, roughly broken
- 40g chopped tomato
- 100g paneer, crumbled (see recipe above)
- 35g cooked black urad dal
- 30g ricotta
- ½ teaspoon sliced green chilli
- 1 handful of mint leaves, chopped
- 1 handful of coriander leaves, chopped
- 1½ tablespoons golden raisins, chopped
- ⅛ teaspoon spice mix (see recipe above)
- ⅛ teaspoon hot chilli powder
- salt and ground black pepper
- 1–2 teaspoons lemon juice

Owners Mykal and Kate Bartholomew opened Tonka when they could no longer bear to turn people away from their original restaurant, Coda (page 155). The couple fell in love with Indian food during a trip there, and their business partner, chef Adam d'Sylva, grew up with a curry and pasta dish on the dinner table every night, courtesy of an Italian mother and Indian father.

This recipe, borrowed from Italy, is a fine example of Tonka's 'flexible cuisine borders'. Food here is less traditional; it avoids ghee (clarified butter) to reduce the heaviness often associated with Indian cuisine and makes the most of fresh Aussie herbs rarely available in India. 'It's important to us that we are a Melbourne restaurant. And that while we use India as inspiration, we are flexible with produce and the Australian palate,' says Bartholomew.

'What I love about the paneer recipe is that people don't realise you can easily make cheese at home – it's only milk, salt and lemon juice. It's really rewarding for the home cook, but it's also really different. Then stuffed in the zucchini flowers, it's bloody delicious!' Bartholomew recommends serving the stuffed zucchini flowers with a salad of pickled zucchini, breakfast radish and baby watercress.

For the paneer, add the milk and a pinch of salt to a heavy-based saucepan over medium heat. Bring up to a little under the boil (80°C if you have a thermometer), stirring occasionally. Turn off the heat and stir in the lemon juice. In 15–20 minutes the solids will start separating from the whey. Stand for a few more minutes – the curd will have completely separated when the liquid is light yellow in colour.

Line a colander with cheesecloth or muslin. Pour the curds and whey mixture into the colander. Tie the ends of the cloth together and lift to drain off excess liquid. Place a heavy weight over the cloth and drain in the colander for 30 minutes to remove all the whey. The paneer is now ready to use.

For the spice mix, toast all the ingredients in a dry frying pan over medium heat for 1–2 minutes until fragrant and slightly darkened. Cool and grind in a spice grinder. Store in a sealed jar in the pantry for up to 6 months.

→

For the stuffing, heat the oil in a small saucepan and add the curry leaves and kashmiri chilli. Cook briefly until fragrant and crackling. Add the tomato and cook until softened, about 3 minutes. Set aside for a few minutes to cool. Add the tomato mix and other stuffing ingredients to a medium bowl with salt, pepper and lemon juice to taste.

Heat a deep-fryer or saucepan of oil to 180°C.

Open the zucchini flowers and remove the stamens. Stuff each flower with about 1½–2 teaspoons of the paneer mixture depending on the size of the flower. Leftover stuffing will keep for 2–3 days in the refrigerator.

Evenly divide the glutinous rice flour, rice flour and tapioca starch between two medium bowls. Dry whisk one of the bowls until combined. Add the soda water to the other bowl and whisk to a smooth batter.

Working in batches, dust each flower lightly in the flour mix and dip in the batter. Fry for 2–3 minutes until golden.

386 Rathdowne Street
Carlton North

Duck Liver Parfait
Gerald's Bar

Serves 6

250g cleaned and trimmed duck livers, at room temperature

300ml port, reduced to 100ml, warm

2 egg yolks, at room temperature

1 egg, at room temperature

250g unsalted butter, clarified and warm

salt flakes and freshly ground white pepper

extra-virgin olive oil, to serve

toast, to serve

cornichons, to serve

Not many places make you feel like a local, but Gerald's Bar in Carlton North does. The dimly lit wine bar is full of character and characters, courtesy of owner-operators Gerald Diffey and Mario Di Ienno. 'It's about eye candy,' says Di Ienno, referring to the eclectic array of decorations. Most of it comes from Diffey's collection, but staff and regulars have contributed over the years, too.

'People tend to go, "we'll just go down for a quick drink" and then suddenly ... Walking in is easy. Leaving is hard,' says Di Ienno. The luscious Duck Liver Parfait – best enjoyed with wine – is one reason why.

'It came about from spending time in France and Spain and enjoying far too much foie gras. We wanted a nice alternative we could serve in Australia. It's a lovely, convivial thing to share. It just fits entirely with what we do,' he says.

For best results, clarify your butter the day before so you can wash the milk solids off the top, rather than skim them from the surface of a pot and miss bits. Ensure everything is at room temperature before cooking so the ingredients don't separate when combined. Serve with something acidic, such as cornichons, to cut through the fat. To store, put the parfait into sterilised glass jars and seal with either butter or duck fat. It will keep in the fridge for up to a month.

Preheat the oven to 115°C fan-forced (130°C conventional).

Using a food processor, puree the livers and port until smooth. With the motor running, add the egg yolks and egg and pour in the butter in a steady stream. Strain the mix through a fine sieve into a jug and season with salt and white pepper.

Pour the mixture into six ceramic bowls or ramekins and place in a deep baking tray. Pour hot water in the tray until halfway up the ramekins and place in the oven for 12–15 minutes until the parfait is just set. Refrigerate for at least 2 hours before serving.

Drizzle the parfaits with olive oil, sprinkle with salt flakes and serve with the toast and cornichons.

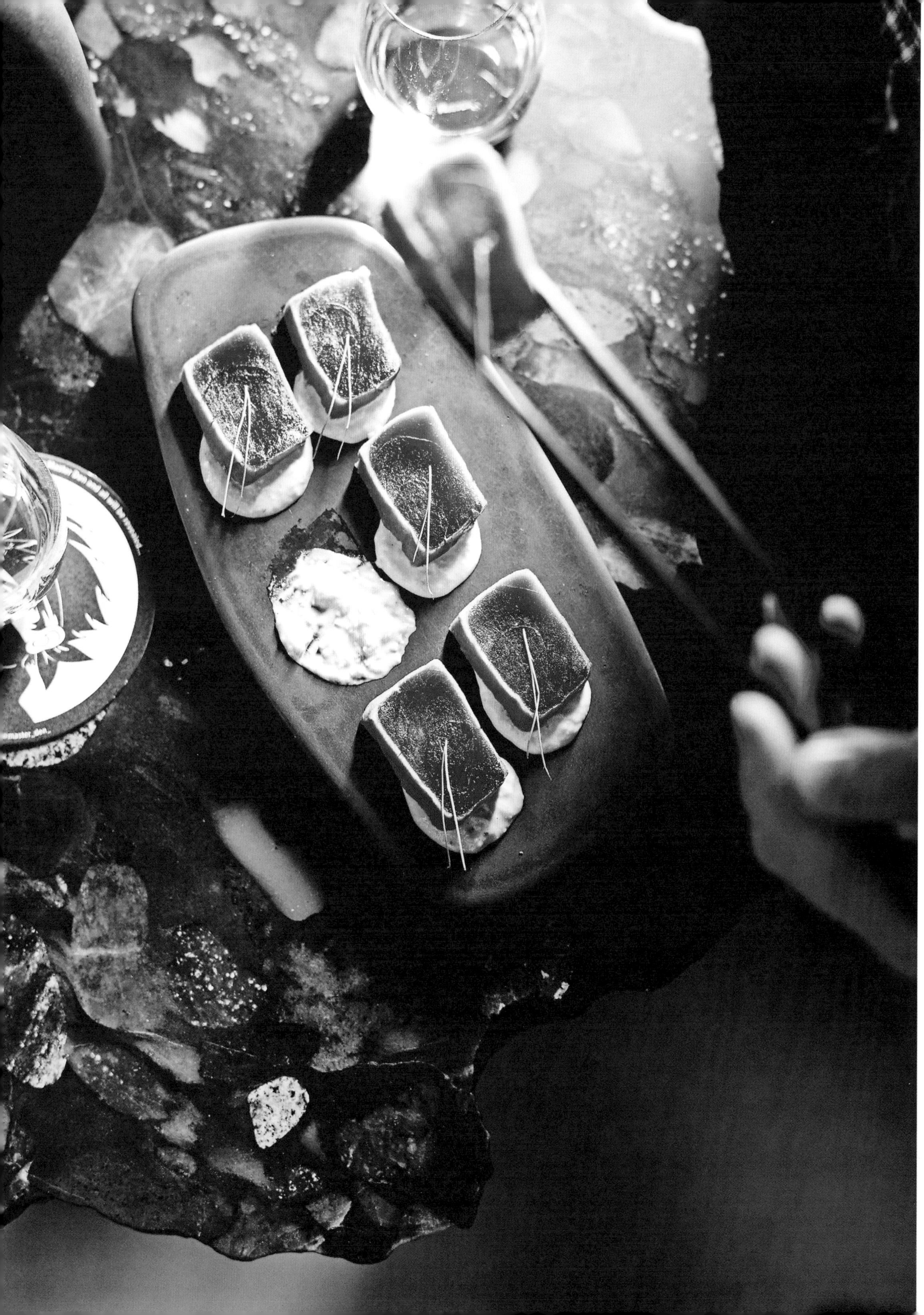

114 Russell Street
Melbourne

Spicy Tuna Tataki
Izakaya Den

Serves 6 as an entree

600g sashimi-grade yellowfin tuna, trimmed square (ask your fishmonger to do this)

3 tablespoons white sesame oil

2 garlic cloves, peeled

½ brown onion, roughly diced

2 hard-boiled eggs

100g Kewpie mayonnaise

½ teaspoon dried parsley

1½ teaspoons wasabi paste

1 teaspoon chilli bean paste (toban djan)

baby chives, to serve

Marinade

125ml mirin

125ml cooking sake

250ml light soy sauce

2 teaspoons bonito flakes

'I thought the Japanese options in Melbourne were not really representative of what we saw when we went to Japan,' says Simon Denton of Izakaya Den, Kappo and Hihou. He saw a gap in the market for relaxed yet authentic Japanese food and, in 2009, decided to open Izakaya Den with his business partners. This Spicy Tuna Tataki recipe has been on the menu since day one. 'When we were doing our food trials it was one of the first dishes we passed for the menu. Some of us liked the wasabi mayo and some of us liked the chilli mayo so we said, "why don't we just do both?"' explains Denton.

The two varieties of tartare can be made in advance, while the tuna can be seared an hour before serving – although Denton recommends slicing it just before plating to preserve the rich colour of the tuna. 'The rim of the seared part and the red flesh in the centre is really beautiful to look at. As they say with Japanese food, you eat with your eyes first.' The tuna has to be sashimi grade, otherwise you can substitute it for swordfish or bonito, which has a more distinct flavour and is popular throughout Japan.

This recipe will need to be started the day before serving.

For the marinade, add the mirin and sake to a small saucepan and heat until the alcohol evaporates, about 1–2 minutes. Stir through the soy and bonito flakes. Pour the marinade into a container, cover and refrigerate overnight.

The next day, slice the tuna lengthways into two rectangular pieces.

Heat the oil in a frying pan over low heat and add the garlic cloves. Once the garlic has browned, lift out of the oil and add to the marinade. Increase the heat to medium–high and sear the tuna for 5 seconds on each side. Add the tuna to the marinade and refrigerate for 4 hours.

Add the onion and eggs to a food processor and process until finely chopped. Mix in the mayonnaise and dried parsley. Divide the tartare between two small bowls and stir the wasabi through one and the chilli paste through the other. Cut the tuna into 5mm-thick slices.

To serve, add a dollop of tartare to each plate for each slice of tuna, alternating between the two sauces. Garnish with the baby chives and serve.

141 Flinders Lane
Melbourne

Sugarcane Prawns with Sweet Chilli Sauce
Coda

Serves 4 (3 per serve)

- vegetable oil, for frying
- 2 garlic cloves
- 3cm piece of ginger
- ½ stalk lemongrass, white part only
- 1 long green chilli
- 300g prawn cutlets, tails removed
- 2 teaspoons oyster sauce
- 2 teaspoons fish sauce
- 1 teaspoon caster sugar
- 1 small handful of coriander leaves
- 1 stick of fresh sugarcane, cut into 12 x 10cm x 1cm sticks
- 100g mung bean noodles, cut into 2–3cm lengths

Sweet chilli sauce (makes about 1½ cups)

- 100g long red chillies, deseeded
- 1 garlic clove
- 3cm piece of ginger
- 1 cup caster sugar
- 125ml rice wine vinegar
- 1 teaspoon salt flakes

Ever since Coda took its sugarcane prawns off the menu, customers have been asking for them back. The balls of sweet-and-sour prawn meat are surrounded by crisp mung bean noodles resembling the hair of a mad scientist, complete with a stick of sugarcane jutting out for easy eating and added sweetness.

'When I'm waiting tables everyone grabs me and says, "What's that?" and I tell them, "Oh it's our sugarcane prawns," and they say, "We'll have four!" It's visually appealing, interesting and easy to do at home. You can impress without going to too much trouble,' says Kate Bartholomew, who owns Coda (and Tonka, page 147) with husband Mykal and chef Adam d'Sylva.

Signature dishes such as these came about after the couple was set on opening a smart-casual French restaurant, but d'Sylva was adamant about cooking Asian food because he had just returned from Vietnam. They ended up with a French-Vietnamese hybrid and what Kate describes affectionately as 'the weirdest menu I've every worked with'.

To make the sweet chilli sauce, add the chillies, garlic and ginger to a blender and blend until smooth. Combine the sugar, vinegar and 125ml of water in a small saucepan and bring to a gentle boil. Add the chilli mixture and salt and simmer for 5 minutes. Set aside to cool. Refrigerate leftover sweet chilli sauce in an airtight container or jar for up to 5 days.

Preheat a deep-fryer or large saucepan of oil to 180°C.

Using a mortar and pestle, pound the garlic, ginger, lemongrass and chilli to form a smooth paste.

Add the paste to a blender with the prawns, oyster sauce, fish sauce, sugar and coriander and blend until smooth.

Mould the prawn mix around the sugarcane sticks, roll in the noodles and fry until crisp, about 2 minutes.

Serve the sugarcane prawns with the sweet chilli sauce on the side.

243 High Street
Northcote

Heritage Tomato, Burrata and Black Garlic
Estelle Bistro

Serves 6

1kg very ripe roma tomatoes

1 bunch of basil, leaves picked and stalks reserved

¼ teaspoon tabasco sauce

salt flakes and freshly ground black pepper

agar agar (the amount required is variable, but you will only need a few grams)

2kg heritage tomatoes (Japanese black, green zebra, white wonder etc.)

3 burrata

1 cup croutons

Black garlic dressing (makes about 500 ml)

250ml red wine

400ml balsamic vinegar

2½ tablespoons red wine vinegar

2 black garlic bulbs, peeled

200ml vegetable oil

200ml extra-virgin olive oil

salt flakes

'We do a heritage tomato dish every year for that lovely six to ten-week period that they're available. To me they're a celebration of summer, whether it's a salad or tomatoes on toast or a gazpacho,' says chef Scott Pickett. Pickett says you can make the recipe throughout the year so long as you source quality roma, vine-ripened or cherry tomatoes in the place of the heritage tomatoes. 'Buy the best, ripest, juiciest tomatoes you can, and always season them separately in a bowl; they just absorb the salt and the oil better and the dressing coats everything.'

This recipe will need to be started the day before serving. You will need a high-powered blender, such as a Thermomix, to make the gel in this recipe.

Add the roma tomatoes, basil stalks and tabasco to a blender or food processor, season with salt and pepper and process to a pulp. Tie the pulp in muslin and hang over a bowl overnight in the refrigerator to catch the tomato water. Once drained, you will have a clear tomato consommé in the bowl. Add the agar agar at a ratio of 1g to 100ml of liquid. Add to a medium saucepan and bring to the boil, whisking constantly. Take off the heat and pass through a fine sieve. Refrigerate until the tomato jelly has set.

To make the black garlic dressing, add the red wine and balsamic to separate small saucepans and reduce over medium–high heat. Reduce the wine to about 50ml, about 8–10 minutes. Reduce the balsamic to a glaze, about 15–20 minutes. Set aside to cool.

Add the reduced wine, balsamic glaze, red wine vinegar and black garlic to a blender and start blending slowly. Drizzle in the vegetable oil and extra-virgin olive oil while blending until smooth. Season with salt. Leftover dressing will keep in the refrigerator for up to 3 weeks and is a great as a salad dressing, drizzled over steamed vegetables or as a glaze for roast lamb.

Blend the set jelly in a high-powered blender (a Thermomix is ideal but don't use a food processor) until a smooth and shiny gel.

Slice the heritage tomatoes into different shapes. Add the tomatoes to a large bowl, dress with a little black garlic dressing and season with salt and pepper.

Place half a burrata ball on each plate, season with a little salt and arrange the tomatoes on top. Tear the basil leaves and scatter over the plate, add a few dots of the tomato jelly and some croutons and serve.

305 St Georges Road
Fitzroy North

Cavolfiore di Gigia (Deep-Fried Cauliflower)
Supermaxi

Serves 4–6

1 tablespoon olive oil

½ red onion, finely sliced

1 tablespoon sherry vinegar

330ml light beer

salt flakes

1¼ cups self-raising flour

½ cauliflower, cut into small florets, stem discarded

oil, for frying

plain flour, for dusting

Getting chef and co-owner of Supermaxi, Rita Macali, to talk about her Fitzroy North restaurant is not easy. She's exceedingly modest, consistently steering conversation away from herself and onto her partner Giovanni Patane, who also runs the restaurant, and her staff. Macali has earned a loyal following for her rustic pizzas and dishes such as the Cavolfiore di Gigia, cauliflower florets fried in batter, which are something her grandmother (and the dish's namesake) used to make.

Macali's nonna's specialty was battered dishes. For Christmas she would make a big bowl of battered salted cod (baccala) and mix it with battered apple pieces. 'They didn't look any different and most of us didn't like the baccala. You'd bite into it and go, "Ugh, I wanted the apple!"' Macali says. 'The cauliflower has broader appeal. It was always a big crowd pleaser and it still is.'

The trick to cooking it like Gigia is to boil the cauliflower for the full 7 minutes. Any less and the flavour isn't released; any more and it will turn to mush. From there, put it aside to cool naturally, resisting the temptation to run it under cold water. 'It's white so you don't have to worry about oxidisation and the colour changing. Adding more water risks it falling to pieces; the less you handle it, the better it is,' says Macali.

Add the olive oil to a small frying pan over medium heat and cook the onion until just softened, about 4 minutes. Add the vinegar and cook until the liquid has been absorbed. Tip out of the pan and set aside.

Add the beer and a pinch of salt to a large bowl and slowly whisk in the self-raising flour until a good batter consistency.

Cook the cauliflower in boiling salted water for 7 minutes. Remove with a slotted spoon and set aside to cool – don't refresh in cold water.

Preheat the oil in a deep-fryer or large saucepan to 175°C.

Dust the cauliflower with a little plain flour and add to the batter. Tap the pieces of cauliflower to remove the excess batter (you want just a nice light coating of batter) and gently lower into the oil in batches. Cook until golden brown, about 4 minutes. Once cooked, remove with a slotted spoon and drain on paper towel. Season to taste while still hot.

Eat the cauliflower hot or cold with the braised onion scattered over the top.

31 Fitzroy Street
St Kilda

La Gricia Sbagliato (Guanciale, Tomato and Chilli Spaghettoni)

Bar Di Stasio

Serves 6

120ml olive oil

100g guanciale, cut into small dice

1 brown onion, diced

2 garlic cloves, crushed

1 bird's eye chilli, finely chopped

500ml tomato passata

250g cherry tomatoes

500g spaghettoni

1 small bunch of basil, leaves picked

1 large handful of flat-leaf parsley, chopped

salt and ground black pepper

freshly grated parmesan, to serve

The restaurateur makes the restaurant. That's the maxim that applies to Rinaldo Di Stasio – Ronnie to his friends – of Bar Di Stasio in St Kilda. The bar next door came 25 years after the original establishment, Cafe Di Stasio, which opened in 1988. In an industry where eateries rise as often as they fall, Di Stasio has become a true Melbourne icon. It's not old school; it's timeless. Ronnie believes in rapport with customers, many of whom he calls friends, food that doesn't need explaining and wine that begs to be finished.

Empty bowls imply that customers care not for explanation when it comes to La Gricia Sbagliato, but home cooks might be interested to know that sbagliato translates to 'incorrect'. This recipe is erroneous in that it's a contemporary version of what shepherds in the Italian mountains would eat for their daily meal. They used only the ingredients most accessible to them other than pasta: sheep and pigs. The former provided the pecorino (a hard cheese) and the latter the guanciale (cured pork jowl). Herbs, seasoning – and some even argue tomato – is technically a bastardisation of the original.

The Di Stasio kitchen recommends using Liguori, Benedetto Cavalieri or Rustichella d'Abruzzo pasta, all of which are made from high-grade durum wheat or semolina by bronze extrusions, which give the pasta a rough and porous surface. This allows the pasta to bind better with the sauce.

Heat a large frying pan over medium–low heat. Add about half the oil and fry the guanciale until lightly golden and crisp, about 4–5 minutes. Remove from the pan, leaving the fat and oil behind, and set aside.

Add the onion to the pan and fry for 4–5 minutes until softened and translucent. Add the garlic and chilli and cook for a few seconds until fragrant. Add the passata, cherry tomatoes and guanciale and simmer gently until the sauce thickens, about 5–8 minutes.

Meanwhile, cook the pasta for 8–10 minutes in plenty of boiling salted water until al dente.

Drain the pasta and add it to the sauce. Add the basil, parsley and remaining oil and toss to combine. Season and serve with the parmesan on the side.

Tonka, Melbourne

Coda, Melbourne

Coda, Melbourne

Izakaya Den, Melbourne

822 High Street
Thornbury

Ragù di Vitello (Veal Ragu)
Umberto Espresso Bar

Serves 6

1kg veal shoulder, cut into 2cm dice

½ brown onion, finely chopped

1 carrot, finely chopped

½ red capsicum, finely chopped

¼ bunch of thyme

2 garlic cloves, crushed

150ml extra-virgin olive oil

1 teaspoon tomato paste

100ml white wine

250g crushed tomatoes

100ml red wine

salt flakes and freshly ground black pepper

750g spaccatelle or bucatini pasta

grated grana padano cheese, to serve (don't substitute with powdered parmesan, it will ruin all your hard work)

It's easy to walk past Umberto Espresso Bar in High Street, but if you did, you'd miss the warm welcome from owner Marco Finanzio. His Calabrian father, Umberto, has lived in Thornbury for more than 50 years.

Past the espresso bar and hanging salumi (made by Umberto) is a courtyard. Here you'll join young families and old friends, the kind who have been around long enough to remember the days when Umberto would visit the local espresso bar – mini Marco in tow – and talk about his dream to open a little Italian restaurant.

This busy Italian restaurant is known for dishes such as Ragù di Vitello, a tomato-based veal sauce served on pasta. 'There's no romantic story about the recipe being passed down to me,' says Marco, 'I just love a slow-cooked, really tender pasta sauce with meat and a tomato base.' As a general rule, the longer you cook it for, the better it gets. Marco recommends leaving it an extra half an hour if you have time: 'The results are always outstanding.'

'We have people eating it on a 40-degree day and they're sweating over it!' he says.

This recipe will need to be started the day before serving.

Add the veal, onion, carrot, capsicum, thyme, garlic and 100ml of oil to a large bowl. Toss to coat and refrigerate overnight.

The next day, heat a large saucepan over high heat and add the remaining oil. Add a handful of the marinated veal to the hot pan and cook until golden brown. Remove and repeat for the remaining veal.

Add the tomato paste to the pan and deglaze with the white wine. Add the veal back to the pan with the tomatoes and red wine. Season and bring to the boil. Reduce the heat to low and simmer for about 2 hours until the meat is falling apart.

Cook the pasta in plenty of boiling salted water until al dente. Drain and add the pasta back to the saucepan, tip in the ragu and stir through.

Serve the pasta with a generous amount of grana padano on the side.

19–21 Lincoln Square South
Carlton

Gnocchi Sorrentina
Kaprica

Serves 6

80ml extra-virgin olive oil

1 teaspoon chopped garlic

1 handful of basil leaves

1kg canned diced tomatoes

salt flakes

200g parmesan, grated

450g buffalo mozzarella, chopped

Gnocchi

800g desiree potatoes, skin on

salt flakes

1 egg yolk

200g type '00' flour

'I've been working in hospitality for over 30 years. You kind of fall in and out of love with it,' admits Pietro Barbagallo. 'But I've fallen back in love with being in the kitchen again and that's because I enjoy the craft of pasta and making gnocchi.' Customers in the know order it regularly: fluffy pillows in a pool of basil-infused tomato sugo, sprinkled with parmesan and mozzarella. It arrives hot from the oven, the cheese melted into a chewy, indulgent mess.

Barbagallo, who made a name for himself in Melbourne making pizza at I Carusi, says it's been difficult to turn the spotlight from pizza to pasta. When he opened Kaprica in Carlton in 2012, his gnocchi was the only pasta dish on the menu. For this recipe the chef recommends using desiree potatoes, which are fairly floury. Avoid placing the potatoes in a food processor otherwise the dough will become sticky.

Start with the gnocchi. Cook the potatoes in boiling salted water until tender and the skins are starting to split, about 30–35 minutes. Drain well.

Meanwhile, to make the sugo, heat the oil in a medium saucepan over medium–low heat. Add the garlic and basil and cook until fragrant. Add the tomatoes, season and simmer for 25–30 minutes. Once cooked, adjust the seasoning if necessary and tip into a large baking dish.

Bring a large saucepan of salted water to the boil – it's important to have this ready to cook the gnocchi as soon as they're made.

Preheat the oven to 180°C fan-forced (200° conventional).

Using a tea towel or gloves, peel the potatoes while still hot and pass through a potato ricer. Add a pinch of salt, the egg yolk and three-quarters of the flour and bring together into a dough, adding a little of the remaining flour if needed. Dust the bench with flour and roll the dough into logs about 2cm thick. Cut each log into 3–4cm pieces and place in a fine sieve to shake off any excess flour.

Working in batches, cook the gnocchi in the boiling water. Once they have risen to the surface, remove with a slotted spoon, briefly drain and add to the sugo in the baking dish. Repeat for the remaining gnocchi, making sure that the water comes back to the boil each time.

Gently mix the gnocchi through the sugo, sprinkle over the parmesan to taste, scatter over the buffalo mozzarella and bake for 10–12 minutes until the mozzarella has melted.

116 Lygon Street
Brunswick East

Persian Meatballs in Saffron and Tomato Sauce
Rumi

Serves 6

500g lamb mince

½ cup medium grain rice, boiled until just cooked

1 egg

1 small brown onion, grated

½ bunch of flat-leaf parsley, leaves picked and finely chopped

1 teaspoon advieh (Persian spice mix, available from Mediterranean and Middle Eastern grocers)

salt flakes

labna, to serve

Sauce

100ml olive oil

1 brown onion, finely diced

10 saffron threads, crushed

1kg canned diced tomatoes

salt flakes

'My sons love them, particularly my second boy; we have to slow him down when we eat at Rumi, he easily puts away six,' says chef and restaurant owner, Joseph Abboud. His Persian meatballs are traditionally bigger than your average – 45 grams, a little larger than a golf ball.

'The boiled rice is what makes it really special,' says Abboud. 'It makes them succulent and soft and that's a particularly Persian way of doing meatballs.' The recipe calls for advieh, a Persian spice mixture that, 'virtually includes every spice you can think of' including more unusual ingredients such as dried rose, lime and golpar, a bitter Iranian plant. Rumi makes 10-kilogram batches of the stuff at a time, but it's a lot easier to buy it from a Mediterranean grocer. 'I probably should put it in jars and put a Rumi sticker on it, because people are always interested in buying it,' jokes Abboud.

When asked if Rumi's popularity stems from the effort that goes into dishes such as the meatballs, Abboud admits he's still trying to work it out. 'Most beautiful things in the world you can't put your finger on.'

To make the meatballs, mix all the ingredients in a large bowl and season. Divide the mix into 45–50g portions, roll into balls and refrigerate while you make the sauce.

To make the sauce, add the oil to a wide-based saucepan large enough to hold the meatballs. Cook the onion over low heat for about 10 minutes until translucent and softened. Add the saffron and cook for 1 minute. Add the tomatoes and cook over low–medium heat for 30 minutes. Season the sauce to taste.

Gently drop the meatballs into the sauce and turn the heat up to high so that the sauce returns to the boil. Turn the heat down to a simmer and cook for 30 minutes.

Serve the meatballs with a dollop of labna.

99 Lygon Street
Brunswick East

Margherita Pizza
400 Gradi

Makes 8 pizzas

800g peeled San Marzano tomatoes, crushed by hand and seasoned to taste

8 buffalo mozzarella balls

1 handful of fresh basil leaves

extra-virgin olive oil

Pizza dough

30g fine sea salt

1kg type '00' flour, sifted

1–3g fresh yeast

Right here on this very page is the recipe for the best margherita pizza in the world. Johnny Di Francesco was crowned World Pizza Champion at the Campionato Mondiale Della Pizza for it in 2014 in Parma, Italy. Di Francesco is also the first Australian trained to the Associazione Verace Pizza Napoleonata pizza-making standards and Brunswick East locals have been enjoying his margherita since 2010 at his Lygon Street institution.

To replicate his version as closely as possible, you'll need a wood-fired oven, peeled tomatoes and DOP-certified buffalo mozzarella. Make sure the base is less than 35 centimetres in diameter and that the edges don't rise more than 2 centimetres. In a conventional oven, Di Francesco recommends using a pizza stone. 'It really does make a difference,' he says. 'And give yourself enough time to let the dough rise properly – don't rush.' The rule with toppings is simple: 'Go for quality every time. There aren't a great deal of toppings on a margherita, so they all need to shine. The pizza should emerge with a soft, pliable base. Leave the cutlery and eat it with your hands.'

This recipe will need to be started 1–2 days before serving.

For the dough, add the salt and 600ml of water to a large bowl and stir until dissolved. Add about a tenth of the flour and mix well. Gradually add more flour and the yeast while mixing. Mix until all the flour is incorporated into a dough. Turn the dough out onto a lightly floured benchtop and knead until smooth and elastic. This can take up to 10 minutes. Place the dough in a lightly floured bowl, cover with a damp tea towel and set aside. Allow the dough to rest for half an hour, but preferably overnight.

Divide the rested dough into eight balls, cover with a damp tea towel and set aside to prove. They can take up to 10–12 hours to double in size.

Preheat the oven to 230°C fan-forced (250°C conventional), or, ideally, heat a wood-fired oven to 400°C. If using a standard oven, preheat a pizza stone until ready to cook.

Once the dough balls have doubled in size, place one on a lightly floured benchtop and stretch by hand to flatten. Roll out the base, or stretch by hand. Spread 100g of tomato across the pizza and top with one ball of mozzarella torn into pieces. Scatter four basil leaves on top and drizzle with some oil. Bake on the pizza stone for 10 minutes, longer if you like it crispier – 90 seconds is enough in a wood-fired oven – and serve immediately. Repeat for the remaining pizzas.

295 Drummond Street
Carlton

Two Pizzas To Make at Home (Yellow Passata, Caciocavallo, Guanciale and Italian Sausage and Chicory, Lemon, Gorgonzola and Mozzarella)

DOC Pizza & Mozzarella Bar

There are multiple pizzas in Melbourne that rival the best in Naples but DOC's thin crust pizzas have become some of the most renowned. Owner Tony Nicolini estimates they make upwards of 10,000 pizzas per week across five locations. 'Creating a DOC pizza at home is as much about the process as it is the finished product,' says Nicolini. 'Get loved ones involved; at DOC we believe this is the most vital ingredient.' Nicolini also recommends no more than four toppings to avoid overcomplicating your pizza. 'Use seasonal flavours – that will narrow down the choices. And be adventurous.'

Makes 8 pizzas

Pizza dough (makes 8 bases)

15g fresh yeast

700ml water, at room temperature

2½ tablespoons extra-virgin olive oil

25g salt flakes

1kg pizza flour

Pizza 1: yellow tomato passata, caciocavallo, guanciale and Italian sausage (topping will cover 4 pizzas)

250g yellow tomatoes

1 pinch of salt flakes

1½ teaspoons chopped oregano leaves

1 tablespoon extra-virgin olive oil, plus extra

300g caciocavallo cheese, shredded

200g Italian sausage, casing removed

150g guanciale, diced

chopped rosemary and thyme leaves, to serve

Pizza 2: chicory, lemon, gorgonzola and mozzarella (topping will cover 4 pizzas)

2 bunches of chicory, chopped into 2cm pieces

extra-virgin olive oil

350g fresh mozzarella

200g gorgonzola

1 lemon, sliced

For the dough, dissolve the yeast in 125ml of the water. Add to a large bowl with the remaining water, oil and salt and mix until the salt and yeast have completely dissolved. Add half the flour and start mixing until you have a soft and quite liquid dough. Add the rest of the flour and keep mixing until the dough forms one soft and smooth ball. Cover with a tea towel and rest for a minimum of 30 minutes.

Once rested, portion the dough and set aside to rise for 2–3 hours, covered. The dough balls should weigh about 200–250g for a standard round pizza, or 650–700g for a 40cm x 20cm rectangular pizza. Adjust based on the size of your pizza tray.

Preheat the oven to 185°C fan-forced (205°C conventional).

For pizza 1's yellow tomato passata, hand crush the tomatoes and mix with the salt, oregano and 1 tablespoon of oil.

For pizza 2, pan-fry the chicory in a little oil over medium–high heat until wilted.

Place a dough ball on an oiled pizza tray and slowly open out with your fingers to cover the tray until about 1cm thick – if the dough is too elastic, rest for a few more minutes. You can also use a rolling pin to roll out the base, but you'll need to rest it for at least 30 minutes before topping.

For pizza 1, spread the yellow tomato passata across the base and rest for a few minutes. Drizzle over a little olive oil and bake for 10 minutes. Scatter over the other ingredients and finish in the oven until cooked completely, about 2–3 minutes. Sprinkle over some rosemary and thyme and serve immediately.

For pizza 2, generously layer the base starting with the mozzarella. Follow with the chicory and gorgonzola and finish with the lemon slices. Bake for 10–15 minutes until nicely cooked.

119 Scotchmer Street
Fitzroy North

Choosing Wine for Your Dish with Paul and Jessica Ghaie of Blackhearts & Sparrows

Paul and Jessica Ghaie are the siblings behind independent bottle shop Blackhearts & Sparrows. With multiple stores across Melbourne, the first of which opened in Windsor in 2005, they're used to suggesting what to drink and when. The idea behind Blackhearts is that anyone can pop in – even if they only have a 20-dollar note in their pocket – and walk out with an interesting and unique bottle of wine.

'Our business was born of the desire to make walking into a specialist wine store less intimidating. Wine can be serious, but most of us associate it with good, fun times, so buying it should reflect this,' says Paul, who believes as much thought should go into a bottle for a special occasion as it does for a movie night at home with takeaway pizza.

'It's fine if the only word you can think of to describe the type of wine you're after is "delicious". Our staff won't bamboozle you with a bunch of wine terms that mean nothing to you. We also have a drinkability scale instore to help make the decision easy, using terms such as "guzzle", "sip" and "impress"', says Paul.

In the last five years Paul and Jessica have noticed an increase in customer requests to help match wine to home cooking. They put it down to people becoming far more experimental with food, both when they eat out and when they're cooking at home. Apparently there's 'no perfect match', but Paul and Jessica have provided us with this cheat sheet to experiment with wine from breakfast through to dessert.

Breakfast

Breakfast is an opportunity to have some fun with drinks and be a little indulgent. Freshly baked pastries are even more decadent when paired with champagne or sparkling wine. The toasty, brioche-like flavours in these beverages will bring out the best in your buttery breakfast.

Pair fresh or poached fruit with the subtle sweetness and light fizz of moscato. Wines with a touch of residual sugar are generally a little lower in alcohol and are ideal for those who don't want to start the day too wobbly.

In the eggs department, chardonnay is the go-to. The fruit spectrum from citrus through to tropical makes it adaptable to all forms of the humble goog. Try light-to-medium styles for basic bacon and eggs through to richer, heavier styles when dealing with hollandaise or crab. Sparkling wine also works well here.

→

Salad and sashimi

Because these dishes are all about lightness, freshness and preserving the purity of the ingredients, the matched wines should be of a similar nature. Delicate, racy, mineral wines, such as sparkling and riesling, work with sashimi, or even a clean, fresh sake. Darker fish can also handle a rosé or a very light-bodied pinot noir.

Wines should complement the robustness of a salad dressing; the acidity in each has to stand up against the other. Try a fresh and zippy sauvignon blanc, pinot grigio or albarino with a green salad or an oxidative, nutty savignan or chardonnay with grain-based salads.

Fried food

The proliferation of burger joints serving delicious greasy things in recent years has encouraged people to give some genuine thought to fried food. Generally, a white with high acidity will help 'de-grease' the palate. Try sparkling or riesling with fish and chips, chenin blanc or a good local sauvignon blanc with soft-shell crab, or gruner veltliner with salt-and-pepper squid. If there's a bit of spice to the food, try a pétillant naturel wine (Pet Nat) – these are left to finish fermenting in the bottle, giving some the tiniest hint of residual sugar and a light fizz (perfect with spicy, fried chicken).

Barbecue

Australian barbecues often – but not always – scream shiraz. Charred meat, whether on its own or in a burger, loves the smoky flavours derived from time in the barrel, so grab a young, oak-aged shiraz with some tannins to help break down the protein, and enjoy the combination of juicy, red fruits with juicy, red meat. Malbec is another variety that has lots of dark fruit flavours and smokiness that marry well with barbecue – just ask the Argentinians. Lagrein and primitivo are some lesser-known varietals that also do justice to this combination.

Spicy food

This is a broad food category and the maturing Australian palate is up to the challenge. Here, Blackhearts & Sparrows suggests choosing a wine with enough flavour to stand up to the spices, but to avoid overly 'oaked' styles because they can dominate the natural fruit. Sweetness and/or fruitiness contrasts against chilli heat and complements the complexity of spices. With reds, choose something low in tannin and made with carbonic maceration, as this process softens tannins and highlights the fruit (go against the grain and slightly chill these reds; it adds an extra cooling effect when paired with chilli-heavy dishes).

White wines to try: off-dry riesling, whether local or from Germany or France; rich, spicy pinot gris or gewürztraminer, particularly from Alsace or New Zealand; field blends commonly involving a mix of riesling, pinot gris and gewürztraminer; or chenin blanc with its honeyed notes and spice profile.

Red wines to try: Gamay from Beaujolais, often made carbonically, is soft and fruity; Barbera from Italy is also good with its gentle but dark fruit flavours and low tannin; or youthful, juicy grenache and shiraz that are bursting with fruit and low in tannin and oak.

Dessert

Sweets can be a minefield for wine matching. The risk is that the drink can overpower the dish. As with most food and wine pairings, the best thing to do is to match the richness of the wine to the richness of the dish. With fruit-based desserts, keep it fresh and fruity with moscato, gewürztraminer, off-dry riesling or chenin blanc. With chocolate, rich and fortified port styles, muscat or a Pedro Ximénez sherry will do the trick. For cream-based desserts, try sweet, rich whites such as botrytis semillon (sauternes), spätlese riesling or rich gewürztraminer. With anything frozen, it's tricky to pair when your tastebuds are being numbed – an ice wine or a Pedro Ximénez can be good here, but it has to be intense enough to break through the chill.

197 Gertrude Street
Fitzroy

Arroz Negra (Squid-Ink Paella)
Añada

Añada is the physical representation of chef and owner Jesse Gerner's obsession with the food of Andalusia and southern Spain. Since the restaurant opened, his approach has been to respect tradition while taking advantage of Australian produce. The Arroz Negra is Añada's signature dish. 'When buying your seafood for this dish, ask for some fish bones, preferably white-flesh fish bones,' advises Gerner. 'Don't use salmon bones because it will make the stock cloudy and ruin the flavour.'

Serves 2

- 2 tablespoons olive oil
- ½ cup calasparra rice
- 1 teaspoon squid ink
- 100g cleaned squid with tentacles, finely sliced
- 100g cleaned cuttlefish with tentacles, finely sliced
- 100g john dory, cut into 2cm cubes
- 3 mussels, cleaned, de-bearded
- 3 green prawns, peeled and deveined, heads and tails on
- 1 handful of flat-leaf parsley leaves
- extra-virgin olive oil, to serve
- lemon cheeks, to serve

Fish stock

- 1 large white fish skeleton, head and tail attached
- 1 carrot, quartered
- 1 brown onion, quartered
- 1 celery stick, quartered
- 1 ripe tomato, squashed
- 2 fresh bay leaves
- 4 black peppercorns

Sofrito

- 2 tablespoons olive oil
- ½ brown onion, finely diced
- 1 garlic clove, finely sliced
- ½ red capsicum, finely diced
- 1 thyme sprig
- 1 fresh bay leaf
- 1 pinch of ground fennel
- salt and ground black pepper
- 1 large tomato, diced
- 65ml white wine or fino sherry
- ½ teaspoon sweet paprika

You will need a 26cm paella pan for this recipe.

For the fish stock, wash the fish skeleton under cold water, making sure to wash away any blood from the gills. Add to a large saucepan and cover with cold water. Bring to a simmer over medium heat, removing any scum as it floats to the top. Add the remaining ingredients and simmer for 45 minutes. Strain the stock, reserving the liquid.

For the sofrito, heat the oil in a medium, heavy-based saucepan over medium–high heat. Add the onion and fry until softened, about 4–5 minutes. Add the garlic, capsicum, thyme, bay leaf, ground fennel and a good pinch of salt. Cook until the capsicum is sweet and soft, about 4–5 minutes. Add the tomato and wine and simmer for another 20 minutes over low–medium heat, stirring occasionally. Stir in the paprika and season with salt and pepper. The sofrito should be quite thick and rich.

Preheat the oven to 200°C fan-forced (220°C conventional).

Add the stock to a medium saucepan and bring to the boil. Reduce the heat until a slow simmer.

Heat the olive oil in the paella pan over medium heat. Add the rice and ½ cup of sofrito and cook, stirring, for 1 minute to toast the rice slightly. Add 440ml of stock and the squid ink and stir in quickly – this will be the only stirring required. Season, keeping in mind that squid ink is salty. Bring to the boil and place the pan in the oven for 13 minutes.

Season the seafood and place on top of the rice in a single layer, lightly pressing the prawns and mussels into the rice. Place back in the oven for 4–6 minutes until the seafood is cooked. Remove the pan from the oven and stand for a couple of minutes. Finish with the parsley leaves, a drizzle of extra-virgin olive oil, a sprinkling of salt and the lemon cheeks. Serve with a green leaf salad and a nice bottle of white wine.

167 St Georges Road
Fitzroy North

Tandoori Chicken
Horn Please

Serves 4–6

6 chicken thigh fillets

1 litre orange juice

25g thyme sprigs

150ml extra-virgin olive oil, plus extra

juice of 1 lemon

1 small fennel bulb, finely sliced

80g mixed green salad leaves

Marinade

160g plain yoghurt

120ml lemon juice

50g ginger, crushed to a paste

50g garlic, crushed to a paste

2 teaspoons gram flour (chickpea flour)

2 teaspoons salt flakes

1 teaspoon ground coriander

1 teaspoon ground cumin

1 teaspoon garam masala

1 teaspoon ground cardamom

1 teaspoon ground turmeric

½ teaspoon kasoori methi (dried fenugreek leaf)

Mango salsa

1 ripe mango, finely diced

1 carrot, finely julienned

2cm piece of ginger, finely julienned

3 coriander stalks, leaves picked

2 spring onions, finely sliced

1½ teaspoons salt flakes

Chicken tandoori shouldn't be red. It comes as a surprise to Westerners who order the dish at Horn Please, the Indian restaurant originally run by Jessi Singh and his wife Jennifer, who have since sold to their longtime associates Amar and Raj Singh.

'Most restaurants add food colouring to their tandoori chicken and say that cayenne pepper or paprika is responsible for the distinctive colour. Chicken should not be red and ours isn't. There's nothing in a traditional tandoori chicken recipe from India that would make the dish appear red,' says Jennifer.

But Horn Please, named after the hand-painted slogan on the back of vehicles in India, isn't all about sticking to tradition. Although Jessi has remained true to his culinary roots from north India to North Fitzroy, he puts his own spin on classic dishes. Tandoori chicken is traditionally slid off the skewer and served with a mint or yoghurt-based chutney and lemon, but Jessi balances the heat and complex spices with a refreshing salsa.

This recipe will need to be started the day before serving.

To make the marinade, combine all the ingredients in a large bowl.

Trim the fat from the chicken and cut into slightly larger than bite-sized pieces. Add to the marinade and massage into the chicken. Cover and refrigerate for 24 hours.

The next day, preheat the oven to 180°C fan-forced (200° conventional).

To make an orange dressing for the chicken, add the orange juice and thyme to a small saucepan and reduce over low heat until approximately 100ml, about 20–30 minutes. Strain and mix with the extra-virgin olive oil.

Add the marinated chicken to a large casserole dish and roast for 20 minutes.

Meanwhile, make a lemon dressing by combining the lemon juice with an equal quantity of extra-virgin olive oil.

→

की,
एक

For the mango salsa, combine all the ingredients in a medium bowl, dress with a couple of teaspoons of the lemon dressing and stir through gently to combine.

Combine the fennel with the salad leaves.

Remove the cooked chicken from the oven and rest for 5 minutes before combining with the orange dressing.

Spread the salad over a long rectangular serving plate, arrange the chicken on top and pour over the remaining lemon dressing. Sprinkle the mango salsa over the top and serve.

176 Toorak Road
South Yarra

Ants Climbing the Trees (Pork Mince Vermicelli Noodles)
Dainty Sichuan

Serves 4–6 as part of a banquet

2 tablespoons peanut or vegetable oil

50g minced pork

2cm piece of ginger, grated

2 garlic cloves, chopped

1 tablespoon chilli broad bean paste (doubanjiang)

1 teaspoon fermented black beans

250g vermicelli noodles, soaked in cold water for 20 minutes, drained and cut into 20cm lengths

1 teaspoon salt flakes

1 teaspoon sugar

1 teaspoon sesame oil

1 teaspoon chilli oil

4cm spring onion, finely sliced

A funny thing happens when you visit Dainty Sichuan for an authentic Sichuan experience; your mouth turns to magma and you lose the feeling in your lips. The menu promises dishes of chicken, beef and noodles but instead plates piled high with dried peppers arrive. It's only once you start digging that you uncover what you ordered. This, after all, is the authentic Sichuan experience. But aside from the soy milk, which diners gulp for relief, there is hope for those who can't handle the heat: Ants Climbing the Trees.

The dish is a moreish mix of vermicelli noodles and pork mince flavoured with black bean, garlic, sesame oil and ginger. 'We look at the pork mince as ants and the rice vermicelli as trees,' says restaurant manager Mackie Huang. It's a great option for kids who take to the back story and get a kick out of slurping slippery noodles. Ants Climbing the Trees is barely spicy, but those who have their doubts can leave the chilli oil out altogether. Huang recommends serving it with a side of fried or steamed Asian greens.

Heat a wok over medium–high heat. Add the oil and cook the pork until half cooked. Add the ginger, garlic, chilli paste and black beans and stir-fry for 1–2 minutes. Add the vermicelli and stir-fry for 30–40 seconds until dry. Add the salt, sugar, sesame oil and chilli oil and mix through. Top with the spring onion and serve.

1–7 Ferguson Street
Abbotsford

Gang Pah Neur (Jungle Curry with Beef) Jinda Thai

Serves 4 as part of a banquet

500ml chicken stock

2 round Thai eggplants, cut into wedges

4 stalks of green peppercorns (in brine, available from Asian grocers)

10 slices of rhizome (grachai or lesser ginger, available in jars at Asian grocers), finely sliced

2 kaffir lime leaves

5 thin slices of kabocha (Japanese) pumpkin, about 3cm x 6cm

10 slices of bamboo shoot (available canned at Asian grocers)

4 baby corn

¼ cup canned straw mushrooms

½ teaspoon sugar

1 teaspoon fish sauce

100g beef eye fillet, sliced

2 Thai basil stalks, leaves picked

sliced red chilli, to serve

Jungle curry paste (makes about 1 cup)

4 long dried chillies, soaked in water and drained

10 small dried chillies, soaked in water and drained

3 garlic cloves, roughly chopped

3 red shallots, roughly chopped

4 kaffir lime leaves

1cm piece of galangal

50g lemongrass, white part only

1 teaspoon shrimp paste

50g rhizome

'With Thai food, when the family gathers for a meal in the evening, on the table there should be a curry, a stir-fry, a nahm prik, some veggies, some fish and some rice,' explains the owner of Jinda Thai, Premika Tanpapat. 'If you have a jungle curry on the table, the rest of the dishes should not be spicy at all so it is complementary. That's how proper Thai dinner should be done.'

According to Tanpapat, it's the mix of spices and herbs that make a jungle curry unique, not just the chilli. She's lived in Melbourne most of her life, but developed a taste for spicy food before she was 10 years old in Thailand. But while some chilli can be left out, she insists, 'This dish is definitely not for kids!' The jungle curry, available in the restaurant, is one of grandma Jinda's original recipes passed down to her granddaughter.

'The recipe has been passed through the generations. My aunty and uncle adapted it to use local ingredients when they started their Thai restaurant in Melbourne, which has since sold. Now my sister, who is the head chef at Jinda, has adapted it to fit in with our generation,' says Tanpapat. The beef is her sister's spin on the dish, which she says is traditionally served with pork, chicken or prawns.

To make the curry paste, add all the ingredients to a food processor and blend at low speed until a smooth paste forms.

Heat the stock in a medium saucepan over medium heat. Add the eggplant, peppercorns, rhizome, lime leaves, pumpkin, bamboo shoots, corn and mushrooms to the pan. Add 1 tablespoon of curry paste and stir well. Add the sugar and fish sauce and taste – it should taste a bit salty and spicy, adjust if necessary. Turn the heat to high and bring to the boil. Add the beef and cook for 30 seconds – don't overcook.

Garnish the curry with the basil leaves and sliced chilli and serve with rice. Leftover curry paste will keep in the freezer for 1 month.

DAVID'S
FREE DELIVERY
DAVID'S
ESTD. 1999

4 Cecil Place
Prahran

Fat Shanghai Noodles with Pork and Black Vinegar
David's Restaurant

Serves 4

340g lean pork, such as fillet, sliced into 5mm strips

120ml vegetable oil

16 dried shiitake mushrooms, soaked in water for 2 hours, drained and finely sliced

1 garlic clove, sliced

900g pre-cooked udon noodles

25ml dark soy sauce

25ml soy sauce

1 tablespoon black vinegar

½ teaspoon sugar

2 small bunches of bok choy, chopped

chilli oil or chilli sauce and vinegar, to serve

Marinade

2 teaspoons shaoxing wine

1 teaspoon light soy sauce

¼ teaspoon dark soy sauce

1½ teaspoons cornflour

1 pinch of caster sugar

David Zhou's journey began with a small teashop on Chapel Street in the early '90s after he moved to Melbourne from Shanghai. His empire has since grown to include three Oriental Teahouses, two bars (Zhou Zhou and Monkey King) and David's Restaurant, a Prahran favourite. But it wasn't always easy for David, especially when it came to trying to find his treasured black vinegar, so readily available in Shanghai. 'When I first came to Australia I went to Dragon Bowl for yum cha on a Sunday afternoon and they give me this pinkish coloured vinegar. It was really sweet; it was a very strange taste for me. Even though we're all from China, it was very foreign,' he says.

'People are starting to experience the regions of Chinese food. Previously it was mainly Cantonese, now there's lots of northern and southern, but when I was first in Chinatown 20 years ago people had no idea ... Some places serve Shanghai dishes but they use Cantonese vinegar; it just doesn't match.'

These thick noodles are an example of a typical Shanghai dish, eaten both in homes and restaurants. Cooking with the vinegar is the equivalent of squeezing lemon over a dish to add acidity. Growing up with these noodles, the smell of black vinegar always conjures memories for Zhou of eating them with his sister. 'The aroma of this dish is always in my mind. It's very Shanghai.'

For the marinade, combine all the ingredients in a medium bowl.

Add the pork to the marinade, mix well and set aside for 10 minutes.

Heat a wok over high heat. Add 2 tablespoons of oil and stir-fry the pork until browned. Remove the pork and set aside.

Reduce the heat to medium and add the remaining oil. Add the mushrooms and garlic and cook for about 2 minutes. Gently separate the noodles and add to the wok. Add the soy sauces, vinegar and sugar and stir-fry until the noodles are an even, deep-brown colour. You can add more dark soy sauce to improve the colour if you like. Add the bok choy and cook until wilted. Serve immediately with chilli oil or chilli sauce and vinegar on the side.

1/22–26 Corrs Lane
Melbourne

Vegetarian Miso Ramen
Fukuryu Ramen

Serves 6

1 x 400–450g wedge of kabocha (Japanese) pumpkin, skin on

750g cooked ramen noodles (about 400g dried)

1 cup finely sliced leek, white part only, washed thoroughly

1½ cups corn kernels

120g butter

60g enoki mushrooms

3 soy-soaked eggs, halved (6-minute boiled eggs covered with soy sauce and marinated for 1–3 hours, depending on preference)

½ cup toasted pumpkin seeds

2 spring onions, finely sliced

Vegan broth

3–4 x 15cm (370g) green leek tops, washed thoroughly

2 large (270 g) brown onions

vegetable oil

2 (8g) dried shiitake mushrooms

6 (25g) garlic cloves

5cm square kombu (edible kelp)

Miso paste (makes about 450g)

1 tablespoon vegetable oil

1 (85g) small brown onion, finely chopped

5 (20g) garlic cloves, minced

1 bird's eye chilli, finely chopped

2½ tablespoons sake

2½ tablespoons mirin

260g red miso paste

2 tablespoons soy sauce

When Fukuryu Ramen first opened in a laneway off Chinatown at the start of 2014, vegetarian options were not a focus. But due to popular demand the kitchen developed a vegetarian ramen that mimics a typical, meat-based noodle soup with a rich broth. The secret: umami.

'A lot of times what's missing in vegetarian food are depth and richness. In Japan we call it umami, so in order to build more of that we release a different dimension of flavour. That's what gives it the body. Otherwise it would just be a sweet onion soup,' explains chef Atsumi Kondo.

Vegetables are roasted until dark, miso paste is prepared and shiitake mushrooms and kombu accent the flavour. The resulting broth is vegan, but the Fukuryu team recommends freestyling when it comes to choosing toppings (try fried salmon instead of the pumpkin).

This recipe relies on putting in the effort to get the results, but there are shortcuts if you're in a rush. For example, Kondo says that using miso paste from a store instead of making your own is acceptable, but you'll be missing out on bold flavours and complexity. 'The stuff you buy is often mixed white and red miso paste. It's kind of plain, it's not deep and exciting, it's just there. What we're doing with this recipe is elevating it to where people feel like they've achieved something,' she says. 'If friends are over and you want to impress, definitely take the time to put it all together. It will make a big difference.'

Preheat the barbecue grill on high, or heat a large frying pan or griddle pan over medium–high heat.

For the broth, brush the leek tops and onions with a little oil to help conduct the heat better (using too much oil will result in an oily soup) and char on the grill until very dark brown, almost black, about 10–15 minutes.

Add the charred leek and onions, shiitake, garlic and 4 litres of water to a large saucepan and bring to the boil over high heat. Once boiling, reduce to a simmer and cook for 1½ hours until reduced to just over 2 litres – you will need 2.1 litres for six portions (350ml each).

Add the kombu to the reduced broth and simmer for 5 minutes. Remove from the heat and strain. The broth can be made in advance and refrigerated for up to 3 days.

→

For the miso paste, heat a deep-sided frying pan over medium heat. Add the oil, followed by the onion, garlic and chilli. Cook until the onion is translucent, about 5–7 minutes. Add the sake and mirin and reduce for 1 minute. Add the miso paste, mix well and cook for 3 minutes. Add the soy sauce, remove from the heat and mix well. Leftover miso paste can be refrigerated in an airtight container for 10 days, or stored in the freezer for up to 3 months.

Cook the pumpkin in simmering salted water until tender, about 10 minutes. Cool and cut into small 5mm-thick pieces, including the skin, allowing for five pieces per bowl. Grill the pumpkin on the barbecue or in a griddle pan for added flavour, if desired.

Heat the broth in a medium saucepan and add 3½ tablespoons of miso paste per 350ml of broth. Bring to the boil and whisk until combined.

Add the miso soup to the bowls, followed by the noodles. Add five slices of pumpkin to each bowl, top with equal quantities of the remaining ingredients and serve.

312 Drummond Street
Carlton

Toasted Fennel Seed Butter
The Town Mouse

Makes about 250g

½ tablespoon fennel seeds
salt flakes
200g butter, softened
50g crème fraîche

Owner Christian McCabe attributes the success of The Town Mouse to good old-fashioned hospitality. 'You need good food and drinks, but people return to restaurants where they feel a connection. Lots of places may have great food, but they don't make people feel a part of it,' he says.

After selling Matterhorn in New Zealand and coming to Australia, McCabe convinced chef Dave Verheul to join him. 'The big difference between New Zealand and Melbourne is that people follow eating out like a sport here. It's a pastime; they're not just going out because it's someone's birthday, they're going out because it's part of their lifestyle,' says McCabe.

From the moment the house butter with bread is brought to the table the experience at The Town Mouse begins. It could be creamy sesame or umami-loaded seaweed, depending on when you visit. 'We put a lot of effort into our bread and our butter,' says Verheul, who describes the toasted fennel seed variety as 'one of those really nice, nurturing kind of things'.

Moving on to the main of snapper with charred broccoli overleaf, Verheul suggests using young fish for this dish, which is not only more tender but also more sustainable. The sauce is made from the clear juice that usually goes to waste when shucking a clam. Mixed with dijon, basil and olive oil, Verheul has recreated a flavour akin to the salty freshness of ocean spray. The broccoli that sits on top has been charred on the grill, because, 'Everything tastes good from the grill. We like burning things, too, the Australian way,' jokes the Kiwi.

Toast the fennel seeds in a dry frying pan over medium heat until deep golden brown and almost burnt. Grind the seeds in a spice grinder with a pinch of salt.

Add the butter and ground fennel to a blender and blend until smooth. Spoon into a medium bowl and whip in the crème fraîche until combined. Season to taste and refrigerate until needed.

312 Drummond Street
Carlton

Snapper with Charred Broccoli, Clam and Capers
The Town Mouse

Serves 4

1 large head of broccoli

90g table salt

1½ tablespoons olive oil

1 tablespoon vegetable oil

4 x 150g snapper fillets, skin removed

50g butter

300ml fish stock

4 sage leaves

1 fresh bay leaf

100g cornichons, pureed

8 large green mizuna sprigs

Clam and olive oil sauce

250ml clam juice (from shucked raw clams)

1 teaspoon dijon mustard

45ml olive oil

salt flakes

8 basil leaves

Crumb mix

100ml vegetable oil

50g capers, drained and dried in a low oven or dehydrator for 2 hours

50g almonds, toasted and finely chopped

For the clam sauce, warm the clam juice to 60°C in a small saucepan. Add the mustard and combine with a hand-held blender. Add the olive oil and blend until emulsified. Season to taste, add the basil leaves and set aside to infuse for 15 minutes before straining.

Using a sharp knife, carefully shave the dark green nodules off the end of the broccoli and reserve for the crumb mix. Cut the head into quarters, keeping all the stem.

Add 3 litres of water and the table salt to a medium–large saucepan and bring to the boil. Blanch the broccoli until just cooked through, refresh in iced water and drain on paper towel.

Heat a griddle pan until lightly smoking, then brush the broccoli with the olive oil and grill until charred on all sides. Set aside to cool a little before slicing into four pieces each.

For the crumb mix, heat the oil in a frying pan until just smoking. Add the reserved shaved broccoli, but be very careful as it will spit. Cook until golden and crisp, 1–2 minutes. Remove from the oil, season well and drain on paper towel. Once cool, mix with the capers and almonds.

Heat the vegetable oil in a large non-stick frying pan over medium–high heat. Season the snapper well on both sides and sear until a light golden colour. Turn over and add the butter, stock and herbs, bring to a simmer and cook while basting for 2–3 minutes until just cooked. By this time the butter and stock should have reduced to a glaze.

Add a little cornichon puree in two spots on each plate and place the cooked snapper in between. Arrange the charred broccoli on top of the fish, spinkle over the crumb mix, pour a little sauce into the middle and finish with the mizuna.

49 Rathdowne Street
Carlton

Quail with Radicchio, Golden Raisins and Grapes
Epocha

Serves 6

2 garlic cloves, finely sliced

¼ bunch of thyme

150ml olive oil

6 butterflied quails (partially de-boned, ask your butcher to do this)

1 bunch of flat-leaf parsley, leaves picked and finely chopped

1 bunch of chives, finely chopped

2 French shallots, finely sliced

1 head of radicchio, leaves torn

3 tablespoons chopped hazelnuts

Golden raisin puree

75g golden raisins

sherry vinegar, to taste

salt flakes

Pickled grapes

125ml champagne vinegar

25g sugar

18 red seedless grapes, halved

Dressing

2 tablespoons sherry vinegar

25g dijon mustard

80ml olive oil

salt flakes and freshly ground black pepper

Dishes such as this quail recipe embody the coming together of European and Mediterranean flavours at chef Angie Giannakodakis's Carlton restaurant Epocha. 'You'll see elements of Italy, Greece and France in there but you still get those clean, fresh flavours coming through,' says Giannakodakis. The dish is based on the idea of the harvest, where quail is often served in summer at the same time grapes are gathered. Giannakodakis recommends it as a starter with a salad or as a light dinner.

Add the garlic, thyme, oil and quails to a large bowl and toss gently to coat. Marinate for 4 hours minimum, but preferably overnight.

For the raisin puree, add the raisins to a small saucepan and cover with water. Bring to the boil, immediately take off the heat and strain. Add the raisins to a blender and blitz to a puree, adding a little water if it needs loosening. Add vinegar and salt to taste – it should have a sweet and sour profile.

For the pickled grapes, bring the vinegar, 25ml of water and the sugar to the boil. Add the grapes to a small bowl and pour over the hot pickling liquid. Set aside to cool.

To make the dressing, whisk the vinegar and mustard in a small bowl and slowly drizzle in the oil until emulsified. Season to taste. Any leftover dressing will keep well refrigerated.

Heat a large frying pan or griddle pan over high heat. Season the quails and cook for 2–3 minutes, skin-side down, until golden brown. Turn over and just seal the other side, about 1–2 minutes. Rest for 2–3 minutes before assembling.

Mix the herbs and shallots and dress to taste, adjusting the seasoning is necessary.

Spread some raisin puree on each serving plate. Dress the radicchio and arrange on the plates. Place the cooked quails on top. Scatter over the pickled grapes. Sprinkle over 2 teaspoons of chopped hazelnuts per plate and serve.

CHAMPAGNE

51 Gipps Street
Collingwood

Apple Barbecue Sauce-Basted Smoked Chicken
Le Bon Ton

Serves 2

1 x 1.4kg chicken, butterflied

1 bag natural charcoal

1 tablespoon salt

1 tablespoon ground black pepper

2 tablespoons paprika

250ml barbecue sauce (Le Bon Ton makes their own, but use your favourite brand)

250ml apple juice

100g unsalted butter, melted

1kg woodchips or chunks (apple wood, ironbark or hickory), soaked in water for 1 hour

Brine

4 litres water

3 tablespoons cooking salt

3 tablespoons garlic salt

Barbecued chicken is often overshadowed by its fried counterpart, but the free-range chook smoked whole and served in halves at Le Bon Ton is worthy competition. It's brined for 24 hours, dried for a day (it makes the skin sticky so smoke adheres to the flesh), massaged with a poultry rub and smoked for 2 hours over ironbark and cherry wood. Finally, it's dipped-to-order in the house barbecue sauce mixed with apple juice and butter.

'The key to smoking poultry is the brine,' explains Alabama-born and Texas-raised Jeremy Sutphin. 'Salt breaks down the cells in the actual meat and that plumps it up, so when you smoke it or cook it, it stays really moist.'

This recipe will need to be started the day before serving. You will need a barbecue with a lid or a smoker for this recipe.

Add all the brine ingredients to a large saucepan and bring to the boil. Turn off the heat and cool completely before adding the chicken to the brine, making sure that it is completely submerged. Refrigerate overnight.

The next day, remove the chicken from the brine, pat dry and refrigerate, uncovered, to dry out the skin.

Add some charcoal to the barbecue and light with firelighters – the coals will need to be red hot before adding any woodchips.

Meanwhile, combine the salt, pepper and paprika in a small bowl.

Remove the chicken from the refrigerator and generously season with the paprika mix. Set aside for 30 minutes while the charcoal comes up to temperature.

Whisk the barbecue sauce, apple juice and melted butter in a bowl and set aside.

Add a handful of woodchips to the hot coals. Place the chicken in the barbecue or smoker and cover with the lid. Keep adding charcoal and woodchips as needed – but don't open the lid unnecessarily – to maintain the smoke and a temperature of about 115°C. Brush the apple barbecue sauce on the chicken after 1 hour, and again after 1½ hours. By this stage, the chicken should be almost ready – if you have a probe thermometer, you're looking for an internal temperature of 75°C. Once cooked, remove the chicken from the barbecue and brush one last time. Wrap the chicken in foil and rest for 30 minutes before serving.

Le Bon Ton, Collingwood

11 Toorak Road
South Yarra

Cooking Steak
with Géraud Fabre of France-Soir

You will need

- 250–300g grass-fed scotch fillets, or other quality cut
- vegetable oil
- salt flakes and freshly ground black pepper
- barbeque or griddle pan
- tray, for resting

Toorak Road restaurant France-Soir has been around for longer than most. Since it opened in 1986 it has only had two head chefs. The first, Joachim Inacio, was at the helm until 2000, after which Géraud Fabre took over. He had already been working in the kitchen for six years at the time. One of the restaurant's most famous dishes is its classic entrecôte, a premium steak served with frites and salad that's remained on the menu for nearly 30 years. Fabre's take on cooking something similar at home is French in both accent and candour: 'Even if you like beef, if you can afford only to buy the good stuff once a week, that's enough,' he says.

Fabre suggests visiting your local butcher and asking for grass-fed beef because, 'cows are meant to eat grass, they're not meant to eat grain. Humans put them onto grain so now they're getting fatter. The marbling in the meat looks better. It tastes good but it's not natural. Imagine if I made you drink beer all day.'

Choose your steak

Before you consider cooking, the first step is choosing your meat. For a great steak, look for good-quality cuts of beef such as eye fillet, entrecôte (porterhouse) or, as in this recipe, scotch fillet (also known as rib eye). The scotch fillet has been chosen for its rich fat content. Head to your local butcher and ask for a grass-fed scotch fillet, then you can start in the kitchen.

→

Prepare the steak

Leave the beef out of the fridge until it reaches room temperature, which will help it cook more quickly and evenly. Preheat the barbecue grill or a griddle pan and make sure it's turned up all the way. Thinly cut the steaks so that they are 2cm thick and between 250–300g. You will notice a small amount of fat in the middle of the scotch fillet; do not remove it or the finished product will have the appearance of a steak with holes in the middle.

Cook the steak

Pat the steak down with vegetable oil and season both sides to taste with salt and pepper. Place it on the barbecue or in the pan and sear each side for a minute. Remove the meat and leave it to rest for 10–30 minutes, uncovered, on something that will allow the juices to drain, like a resting tray with holes in it or an oven grill tray set above a plate. Resting causes the fibres of the meat to relax following the aggravation of the grill, resulting in increased tenderness and flavour release. This is also the time to prepare any sides or sauces.

Char the steak

Reheat the barbecue grill or pan and place the steak back on once the resting time is up. Place it perpendicular to how it was before to create a charred, criss-cross effect. Leave for a minute on each side. This will result in a rare steak, cooked on the outside and blue on the inside, just how Fabre likes it.

The perfect steak for you

If you prefer your steak cooked through a little more, add an extra minute on each side for medium-rare, an extra 2 minutes on each side for medium and for well-done, lower the heat to prevent burning and cook for an extra 3 minutes on each side. It's better to undercook than overcook as you can always put your steak back in the pan or on the grill.

Cumulus Inc.

45 Flinders Lane
Melbourne

'When I was travelling in Spain many years ago I ordered a lamb dish at a small club of some description. It was in Rioja, the wine region, and there were a lot of people sitting around playing cards. When it came out, it was this tiny little lamb shoulder, but it was one of the best things I've ever eaten,' explains Andrew McConnell. Knowing it would make for a fantastic share plate in a restaurant, he refined the idea, increased the size and put it on the menu at Cumulus Inc. The result was fall-off-the-bone flesh with a caramelised crust that remains one of the restaurant's most-ordered dishes. 'We've made a lot of friends with it,' he admits.

But Cumulus Inc. makes as many friends with vegetables as it does with proteins. The Organic Carrots with Almond Cream and Harissa (see page 215) is the perfect accompaniment to the lamb shoulder. McConnell's classic Tuna Tartare with Crushed Pea Salad (see page 216) is a lighter option and relies on the highest quality, sashimi-grade tuna. Fresh peas doused in olive oil and lemon are arranged on a generous smear of goat's curd and then piled high with ruby-red cubes of fish, which have been marinated in soy, olive oil, balsamic, crushed garlic and anchovy.

According to McConnell, there's more to good eating than dining out. 'Often the best food experiences are not necessarily in restaurants,' he says. 'It could be at someone's house or standing outside a nightclub in Shanghai at five o'clock in the morning in the snow eating from a yakitori stand.'

45 Flinders Lane
Melbourne

Whole Slow-Roasted Lamb Shoulder
Cumulus Inc.

Serves 6

1 x 2.5kg lamb shoulder, bone in

lemon cheeks, to serve

Marinade

2 garlic cloves, crushed

finely grated zest of 2 lemons

2 tablespoons finely chopped oregano leaves

3 tablespoons olive oil

2 tablespoons salt flakes, plus extra

Marinated onion

2 red onions, finely sliced lengthways

1 pinch of salt flakes

juice of ½ lemon

2 tablespoons olive oil

1 pinch of ground sumac

1 tablespoon chopped flat-leaf parsley leaves

To make the marinade, combine the garlic, lemon zest, oregano, olive oil and salt in a small bowl.

Place the lamb shoulder in a deep, heavy baking tray and rub the marinade all over the joint. Cover with plastic wrap and set aside for a few hours. If you're planning ahead, the lamb is even better marinated in the refrigerator overnight.

Preheat the oven to 150°C fan-forced (170° conventional).

Uncover the marinated lamb and add 250ml of water to the tray. Cover the whole tray tightly with foil and place in the oven for 2 hours. Turn the temperature down to 110°C fan-forced (130°C conventional) and cook for another 6 hours, adding a little more water to the tray from time to time if necessary. Remove the foil for the last hour of roasting to crisp up the outside.

For the marinated onion, add the onion to a medium bowl and break up the slices with your hands. Add a good pinch of salt, toss and set aside for about 1 hour to soften.

Drain the softened onion and add to a medium bowl. Add the lemon juice, oil, sumac and parsley and combine thoroughly.

The lamb is ready when you can easily pull the meat from the bone with a fork. Place the lamb on a serving platter. Pour the juices from the tray into a small jug and skim off most of the fat. Shred the meat from the bone at the table and serve with the roasting juices, marinated onion, lemon cheeks and extra salt on the side.

45 Flinders Lane
Melbourne

Organic Carrots with Almond Cream and Harissa
Cumulus Inc.

Serves 4

60g butter,
plus 1 teaspoon extra

2 tablespoons flaked almonds

2 bunches of Dutch carrots or 2 large carrots (about 500g), trimmed and scrubbed (don't peel)

Almond cream

100g almond meal

350ml olive oil

1 egg yolk

salt flakes

1 teaspoon sherry vinegar (or to taste)

Harissa

1 red capsicum, roasted, peeled and deseeded

125g long red chillies, deseeded

2 garlic cloves

1 heaped teaspoon ground caraway

1½ heaped teaspoons ground cumin

2 tablespoons olive oil

2 teaspoons red wine vinegar

1 teaspoon smoked paprika

For the almond cream, place the almond meal, 75ml of oil and 150ml of water in a small saucepan and gently heat until just lightly warm. Transfer to a blender, add the egg yolk and puree. With the blender running, slowly pour in the remaining oil and blend until thick and creamy – the texture should be silky smooth and similar to mayonnaise. Season to taste with salt and sherry vinegar.

For the harissa, puree the capsicum in a blender. Tip into a small saucepan over low heat and cook until most of the moisture has evaporated. Set aside to cool. Add the chillies, garlic, caraway, cumin and a pinch of salt to the blender and blend until smooth. Add the capsicum and blend until very smooth. While the blender is running, add the oil, vinegar and paprika. Adjust the seasoning if necessary.

Melt 60g of butter in a small saucepan over low–medium heat. Add the flaked almonds and cook, stirring, until golden, 1–2 minutes. Drain on paper towel and season with a pinch of salt.

Cook the carrots in a large saucepan of boiling salted water until just cooked – they should still be slightly crunchy to the bite. Quickly transfer the carrots to a frying pan and sauté with the extra butter until golden. Tip the carrots into a bowl and toss with 2 tablespoons of the harissa and a pinch of salt until well coated.

Spoon ⅓ cup of almond cream onto a serving platter and smear it across the platter with the back of the spoon. Arrange the carrots over the almond cream and top with another tablespoon of harissa, or to taste. Sprinkle with the toasted flaked almonds and serve.

Leftover almond cream will keep for 4–5 days refrigerated. Leftover harissa will keep in the fridge for 7 days.

45 Flinders Lane
Melbourne

Tuna Tartare with Crushed Pea Salad
Cumulus Inc.

Serves 4 as a shared plate

½ garlic clove

1 anchovy fillet (Cumulus recommends Ortiz brand)

1 tablespoon light soy sauce

1 pinch of caster sugar

2 tablespoons olive oil

1 teaspoon balsamic vinegar

finely grated zest of ¼ lemon

250g sashimi-grade tuna, trimmed

130g peas

3 tablespoons extra-virgin olive oil

1 tablespoon lemon juice

1 spring onion, finely sliced

20 mint leaves, shredded

salt flakes and freshly ground white pepper

3 tablespoons goat's curd

8 pea tendrils

rocket flowers, to serve

Using a mortar and pestle, crush the garlic and anchovy to a paste. Transfer to a medium bowl and whisk in the soy sauce, sugar, olive oil, vinegar and lemon zest.

Cut the tuna into 1cm cubes and place in the bowl with the dressing. Marinate in the refrigerator for 15 minutes, stirring gently every so often.

Meanwhile, bring 2 litres of salted water to the boil and blanch the peas for about 2 minutes until tender. Refresh in iced water, drain and crush gently using a mortar and pestle.

Add the crushed peas to a medium bowl with the extra-virgin olive oil, lemon juice, spring onion and mint. Mix well and season with salt and white pepper to taste.

To serve, use the back of a spoon to spread the goat's curd over a serving plate and arrange the crushed pea salad on top. Season the tuna with a pinch of salt and, using a slotted spoon, remove the tuna from the marinade and carefully arrange over the pea salad. Dress the plate with pea tendrils and rocket flowers and serve.

Pidapipó, Carlton

Dessert

→

T. Cavallaro & Sons, Footscray

BUDGET TIN
Ord

273 Hawthorn Road
Caulfield North

Salted Caramel Milkshake
Tuck Shop Take Away

Serves 6

220ml cream

270g caster sugar

60g light corn syrup

70g unsalted butter

2 teaspoons salt flakes

200ml very cold milk, plus about 2 litres to serve

They don't make milk bars like they used to, but we don't mind when they come like Tuck Shop Take Away. This Caulfield cafe mixes nostalgia with experience. Between them, husband-and-wife team Clinton and Karina Serex have worked at The Fat Duck in the UK, Vue de Monde and Attica.

The milkshakes here use house-made syrups and range from redskin to milko, but the original salted caramel – no longer available instore – is our pick. 'The thing about milkshakes is that big kids enjoy them – like you and me,' says Karina. 'For us, it's just about trying to conjure up that nostalgia.' Salted caramel is made from scratch so the sweetness can be manipulated. Ice cream is never added to avoid spiking that sugar and diluting the flavour. Karina admits the salted caramel milkshake is a bit naughty and most appropriate for a weekend treat.

Heat the cream in a microwave-safe jug on medium for 1 minute.

Add the sugar, corn syrup and 100ml of water to a medium saucepan and bring to the boil. Cook until a golden caramel colour and take off the heat. Add the cream carefully – it will froth up – and whisk to incorporate. Whisk in the butter and salt until smooth. Set aside to cool.

Once cooled to room temperature, whisk in 200ml of milk. The salted caramel can be stored in the fridge until needed.

Make sure your milk is super cold when serving. To serve, place a milkshake cup on a set of scales and weigh out 120g of salted caramel and 330g of milk. Mix with a milkshake maker, blender or hand-held blender until frothy. Serve in a chilled milkshake glass and repeat as needed.

98 Hopkins Street
Footscray

Zuddi
T. Cavallaro & Sons

Makes 50–60 biscuits

600g caster sugar

200g unsalted butter, at room temperature

5 eggs, plus 1 beaten egg for brushing

300g blanched almonds, chopped

25g orange zest, chopped

800g plain flour

40g baking powder

Anthony Cavallaro – or Tony to the locals – was born in Footscray after his father migrated to Australia in 1949. Seven years after the move, T. Cavallaro & Sons opened on Hopkins Street selling sweet Sicilian specialties, just in time for the Melbourne Olympics. 'Probably the thing that keeps us in business is the fact that we haven't diverted from the things dad implemented; we're still true to our heritage in that we do things by hand and we keep it that way,' says Cavallaro.

This includes sourcing New Zealand corn flour for its famed cannoli (a secret recipe that Tony couldn't part with) and blanching and crushing its own almonds for almond biscotti. This recipe for zuddi, which dates back to the late 1800s, has been passed down from Cavallaro's grandfather. It's incredibly straightforward and perfect with coffee (a short black in the morning followed by a latte or cappuccino, if you're a true Italian). Tony suggests dipping them in chocolate if you're feeling decadent.

Preheat the oven to 180°C fan-forced (200°C conventional). Line two baking trays with baking paper.

Cream the sugar, butter and 5 eggs on low speed with an electric mixer for 4–5 minutes until smooth. Add the almonds, 2½ teaspoons of water and the orange zest and combine. Add the flour and baking powder and mix until combined.

Roll out the dough into several logs and flatten to 1cm thick, then cut into 6cm x 8cm strips. Brush the surface lightly with the beaten egg. Arrange on the prepared trays with space between each, as they will spread when baking, and bake for 8–10 minutes.

Note that the zuddi dough can be wrapped in plastic wrap and frozen in an airtight container or snaplock bag for up to 3 months. Simply thaw in the refrigerator overnight before baking.

BAKER D. CHIRICO
GRANOLA MUESLI
LEMON TEA CAKE $5.50
PORTUGUESE TART $1.00
PORK & FENNEL CALZONE $9.00
BAKER D. CHIRICO

Baker D. Chirico

178 Faraday Street
Carlton

Daniel Chirico focuses on providing a boutique experience and attention to detail, from the nougat packaging to the bread and the sweet, delicate cannoli overleaf. Around a dozen of the latter are made first thing in the morning and then restocked, fresh, as each lot inevitably sells out.

'The recipe is inspired by the town where my dad was born, in Calabria in Italy. Taurianova is a little town well known for its pastry shops. In particular, the cannoli there are just amazing,' says Chirico. 'They're just plain with blended sheep's milk and cow's milk ricotta and a little bit of lemon zest. They're just unbelievable. It's overwhelming, I can't even explain it to you; you have to sit down and eat one.'

Sheep's milk is more difficult to get hold of in Australia, but one of Chirico's former pastry chefs, Marianna DiBartolo (of Dolcetti in West Melbourne), is Sicilian and knows a thing or two about cannoli. 'Marianna and I put our recipes together and created our own version,' says Chirico. It's important to have clean, quality oil (such as cottonseed) that can be heated to a high temperature. That way the pastry shells don't need to sit in it for too long. A firm, non-watery ricotta also helps, which you can buy from La Latteria in Carlton.

178 Faraday Street
Carlton

Sicilian Cannoli
Baker D. Chirico

Makes about 25 cannoli

cottonseed or canola oil, for deep-frying

400g full-fat ricotta

100g pure icing sugar, sifted, plus extra to dust

2 tablespoons finely chopped dark chocolate

2 tablespoons finely chopped maraschino cherries in liqueur (Baker D. uses Luxardo brand)

3 tablespoons finely chopped unsalted pistachios

Cannoli shells

200g plain flour

15g unsalted butter, at room temperature

1½ teaspoons ground cinnamon

1 tablespoon caster sugar

1 pinch of salt flakes

80ml marsala, plus extra

2 egg yolks

This recipe is best started the day before serving. You will need cannoli forms to hold the pastry in shape while frying.

To make the shells, add the flour, butter, cinnamon, sugar and salt to the bowl of a stand mixer and combine using the paddle attachment until a crumb texture. (If doing this by hand, rub the butter into the other ingredients using your fingers.) In a separate bowl, lightly whisk the marsala and the egg yolks. With the mixer running, slowly add most of the marsala and egg mix. Continue adding until the mixture comes together in a firm dough. A little extra marsala may be needed, but the dough shouldn't be too wet. Continue to work the dough in the mixer, or knead by hand on the bench, until a smooth, firm dough is achieved. Flatten the dough, wrap in plastic wrap and refrigerate for at least 2 hours, but preferably overnight.

After resting, roll the dough out to an even 1mm thickness. The easiest way to do this at home is to use a pasta machine. Otherwise, carefully roll the dough with a rolling pin as evenly and thinly as you can. You may need to use some flour to roll this out, but use as little as possible as the dough will dry out easily. Cut the rolled dough into 9cm squares. Bring the scraps together and roll out again until all the dough is used up.

Lightly oil the cannoli forms to prevent the dough sticking. Place a form diagonally across one of the dough squares and wrap it around the tube. Add a tiny dab of water where the corners meet and press down firmly. Repeat for all the cannoli forms.

Add enough oil to a large saucepan to fill it by at least 12cm and heat to 180°C.

Fry the cannoli shells until evenly golden brown and drain on paper towel. It helps to place the shells upright or leaning so that the oil can drain out. Repeat for the remaining cannoli shells.

To make the filling, add the ricotta and icing sugar to a medium bowl and combine with a spatula until smooth. Fold in the chocolate and cherries until evenly distributed and transfer to a piping bag.

To assemble the cannoli, pipe the filling into the cooled shells, dip the ends into the pistachios and dust with the extra icing sugar.

13 Anderson Street
Yarraville

Jam and Custard Doughnuts
Cobb Lane

Makes 16 doughnuts

600g plain flour

60g caster sugar

1½ teaspoons salt flakes

125ml milk

3 tablespoons dark rum

36g fresh yeast

4 eggs

200g unsalted butter, diced, at room temperature

oil, for deep-frying

150g sugar

1 tablespoon ground cinnamon

1 cup raspberry jam

Custard filling

200ml milk

½ vanilla pod, split lengthways, seeds scraped

40g caster sugar

2 egg yolks

2 tablespoons cornflour

Originally from Yorkshire in the UK, Matt Forbes established Cobb Lane in 2013 following his success supplying baked goods to cafes. It was the doughnuts that did it.

'When we started the business we were doing doughnuts for Clement Coffee in South Melbourne Market,' he says. 'It didn't take long before I was getting phone calls every day to see if we could supply other cafes.'

Forbes' number-one rule when making doughnuts is patience. Make the dough the day before and don't rush the proving process. If you do, the result will be dense dough, not the light and fluffy style for which Forbes has become famous. The custard recipe also appears throughout his bakery repertoire in danishes and other pastries. Cornflour results in a thicker-than-usual product, appropriate to load into a pastry base and top with fruit.

'You can flavour it pretty much any way you want: mix it with pistachio paste; infuse the milk with coffee. Afterwards we sometimes use rosewater and orange blossom, too. It's amazing in the base of tarts.' says Forbes.

Add the flour, caster sugar and salt flakes to the bowl of a stand mixer and fit the dough hook.

In a separate bowl, whisk the milk, rum, yeast and eggs until the yeast has fully dissolved. Add to the dry ingredients in the mixer and mix on the lowest speed for about 10 minutes until the dough starts to come away from the side of the bowl. Gradually add the softened butter until fully incorporated, occasionally stopping to scrape down the side of the bowl with a spatula. Continue mixing on low for about 5 minutes until the dough is smooth and shiny. Remove the bowl from the mixer and cover with plastic wrap. Set aside at room temperature until the dough doubles in size, about 1½ hours.

Line a tray with greased baking paper.

Turn the risen dough out onto a floured benchtop and knead lightly for a minute or so – this process is known as knocking back. Using a rolling pin, roll out the dough to an even 3cm thickness and cut out rounds using a 7cm cookie cutter. Place the rounds on the prepared tray and cover with plastic wrap. Set aside at room temperature until doubled in size, about 1½ hours.

→

Heat the oil in a deep-fryer or large saucepan to 160°C.

Combine the sugar and cinnamon in a deep, flat dish.

Gently place three or four of the risen doughnuts into the hot oil, being careful not to drop them and splash oil on your hands. Cook for 3–3½ minutes on each side until golden. Once cooked, remove from the oil using a slotted spoon and drain on paper towel.

Roll the doughnuts in the cinnamon sugar and, once fully coated, set aside on a tray to cool completely before filling.

To make the custard filling, add the milk and vanilla pod and seeds to a small saucepan. Bring to the boil and remove from the heat. Whisk the sugar and egg yolks in a medium bowl. Once combined, sift in the cornflour slowly while whisking. Pour a third of the hot milk into the bowl while whisking. Pour the mix back into the remaining hot milk in the pan and bring back to the boil while whisking constantly. Once the custard boils, pour it into a bowl and place plastic wrap directly on the custard to avoid a skin forming. Set aside to cool before refrigerating.

Once the custard has cooled completely, remove the vanilla pod and whisk until smooth. You can now add some other flavours if you like, such as rosewater or orange blossom water.

Make a 2cm-wide cut in the side of each doughnut with a sharp paring knife. Fill a piping bag with the custard and pipe a generous amount into the centre, then do the same with the jam.

Ladro, Fitzroy

Cumulus Inc., Melbourne

356 Smith Street
Collingwood

Gluten-Free Chocolate Brownie
Tomboy

Makes 1 x 20 x 30cm brownie slab

- 500g quality dark chocolate, chopped
- 350g butter, diced
- 6 eggs
- 350g caster sugar
- 1 teaspoon vanilla essence
- 200g gluten-free self-raising flour (Tomboy recommends Orgran brand, or try their own recipe opposite)
- ¾ cup raspberries, chopped nougat or melted crunchy peanut butter (optional)

Georgina March was diagnosed with coeliac disease when she was 17 and working at Adelaide Central Market. 'I had such a sweet tooth and I couldn't eat all the sweets around me, so I just started to play around with recipes – it was purely a selfish enterprise, initially,' she says. March moved to Melbourne with Pia Hambour and together they cooked out of an old wood mill in Collingwood, supplying Melbourne coffee spots with gluten-free baked goods before opening Tomboy cafe around the corner, where March continues to run the wholesale enterprise, Box Brownies.

Box Brownie flavours rotate regularly and can include anything from peanut butter and nougat to Murray River salted caramel and Turkish delight. March's original brownie recipe, which she has been perfecting for over a decade, is still our favourite.

March makes her own gluten-free flour by mixing together 200g quinoa flour, 200g millet flour, 300g white rice flour and 300g corn starch (to yield 1kg gluten-free flour, which will keep well in an airtight glass jar). 'A pinch of xanthan gum can aid in binding but is not essential,' she says. The difference between the gluten-free and wheat-based products is noticeable in their consistency – the flavour is still there with the gluten-free brownie but it doesn't sit as heavily in your stomach.

March has a couple of pointers for getting it right: 'I recommend checking the brownies diligently; they're not going to be influenced too much by opening and closing the oven. Check it a little bit early because there are slight heat differences between ovens. You want a skewer to come out and the mix to cling to the skewer, so it's sticky but not wet,' says March.

Preheat the oven to 180°C fan-forced (200°C conventional). Line a 20cm x 30cm baking tin with baking paper.

Add the chocolate and butter to a stainless steel bowl over a saucepan of simmering water. Once mostly melted, stir to combine and take off the heat.

Beat the eggs, sugar and vanilla on low speed with an electric mixer until thick and pale, about 3–4 minutes. Gradually pour the chocolate mixture into the egg mixture while whisking. Whisk in the flour until incorporated. Pour into the prepared tin and top with the raspberries or chopped nougat, or swirl in the peanut butter (if using). Bake for 30–35 minutes until a skewer comes out slightly sticky. Cool before cutting into portions.

Choc Chip Cookie Sandwich with Rosemary Parfait
Pierre Roelofs

Serves 6

Rosemary parfait

3 gold-strength gelatine leaves

50g rosemary sprigs

400g cream (35% fat), plus extra

10 egg yolks

200g caster sugar

⅛ teaspoon salt flakes

Cookies

110g unsalted butter, at room temperature

100g caster sugar

90g soft brown sugar

⅛ teaspoon salt flakes

1 egg

200g plain flour

1 teaspoon baking powder

280g good-quality dark chocolate chips

From turning plates into sugary canvases to his signature layered tubes, Pierre Roelofs' skills in the sweet department have resulted in a loyal following. He learned the ropes during an apprenticeship in the Swiss Alps, before undertaking stints around Europe at Michelin-starred restaurants, including The Fat Duck.

A dessert Roelofs made years ago at a two Michelin-starred restaurant inspired this rosemary and choc chip cookie sandwich. 'The combination of those two flavours I've done in a more elaborate way in the past. I've simplified it here to something the home cook can achieve,' says Roelofs.

Following his time doing weekly dessert degustations at Cafe Rosamond in Fitzroy, Roelofs admits that people have come to expect a certain level of intricacy from him. 'Chefs tend to overcomplicate. It is kind of a cliché, but as you mature in your trade you end up simplifying a lot more. Now, without consciously doing it, I end up topping it at about seven or eight elements, maximum. There are only so many textures and flavours you can perceive in a mouthful,' he says.

This parfait is at the opposite end of the scale to what we expect from Roelofs. He specifically chose parfait instead of ice cream because it doesn't involve an extra piece of equipment. 'I love the idea of having something that's distinctly simple,' he says.

This recipe will need to be started the day before serving. You will need a candy thermometer for this recipe.

For the parfait, add the gelatine leaves to a bowl of cold water to soften.

Line a 30cm x 23cm tray with three layers of plastic wrap – this will ensure that the wrap is robust enough to not tear after freezing.

Break the rosemary sprigs up by hand – this will help to release more flavour into the infusion – and add to a small saucepan with the cream. Bring up to the boil and take straight off the heat. Set aside to steep for 15 minutes. Do not leave any longer, as the rosemary flavour will become too intense.

Strain the rosemary cream, using a ladle to force though as much liquid as possible, into a medium bowl. Cool the cream by placing the bowl in an ice bath, stirring every 5 minutes to help it cool more rapidly.

→

Weigh the cooled cream and top up with fresh cream to bring it up to 400g. Whip to soft peaks and refrigerate.

Add the egg yolks to the bowl of a stand mixer and whisk on high speed.

While the yolks are being whisked, heat the sugar, salt and 1½ tablespoons of water in a small saucepan over medium heat. Swirl the pan until all the sugar dissolves. Once it reaches 121°C, reduce the mixer speed to low and gradually pour in the syrup. This mixture is known as pâte à bombe; it stabilises the yolks and encourages aeration. Once incorporated, increase the speed to full and whisk until cool.

Pour the pâte à bombe into a large bowl, making sure not to scrape any sugar syrup that may have cooled and hardened on the side of the mixing bowl. Use a whisk to fold a third of the whipped cream into the pâte à bombe. Once incorporated, fold in the remaining cream.

Lift the gelatine out of the water and squeeze out any excess liquid with your hands. Melt the gelatine in a small saucepan over very low heat.

Add the melted gelatine to the parfait mixture, mix well and pour into the prepared tray. Spread evenly and check the depth, the ideal thickness is 1.5cm. Excess mixture can be frozen in individual glasses and used as the base for another dessert. Freeze the parfait overnight.

To make the cookies (do this on the day of serving), place the butter, sugars and salt in the bowl of a stand mixer and mix on low speed using the paddle attachment. Add the egg, followed by the flour and baking powder. Once incorporated, add the chocolate chips and mix until evenly distributed. Wrap in plastic wrap and refrigerate for a minimum of 4 hours.

Preheat the oven to 150°C fan-forced (160°C conventional). Line a baking tray with baking paper.

Weigh out twelve 50g portions (or as many as you require) of cookie dough and roll into balls. Place the balls on the prepared tray and squash until about 8cm in diameter. Bake for about 12 minutes, turning the tray once to ensure even baking, until lightly golden. If you'd like a perfectly round cookie use an 8cm cutter to trim the cookies as soon as they come out of the oven. Set aside to cool. The cookies will be pliable and slightly soft once cooled. Any excess cookie dough can be frozen for up to 3 months.

Working quickly, remove the parfait from the tray and use an 8cm round cutter to cut out six circles (or as many as you require). To achieve a clean edge, simply dip the cutter in a bowl of hot water and dry before each cut. Keep the parfait discs in the freezer until ready to serve.

Sandwich the parfait discs between the choc chip cookies and serve immediately.

647 Chapel Street
South Yarra

Classic Chocolate Cake
Burch & Purchese Sweet Studio

Serves 8–12
canola spray
cocoa powder, to dust
5–6 tablespoons apricot jam

Chocolate sponge
4 egg yolks
50g liquid glucose
4 eggs
4 egg whites
30g caster sugar
160g hazelnut meal
150g icing sugar
40g plain flour
40g cornflour
80g cocoa powder
→

'Chocolate cake contains two of the most important food groups, chocolate and cake,' says Darren Purchese, owner of Burch & Purchese Sweet Studio in South Yarra. 'It needs to be moist, rich and have an equal blend of decadent extravagance and the comfort of a hug from mum.'

Given the complexity of his creations (think edible artwork and Lego cakes), he's given us a show-stopper of a chocolate cake with a classic chocolate and hazelnut sponge base that anyone can achieve. There are another five components on top of that – orange syrup, apricot jam, milk chocolate cream, dark chocolate covering and a shiny chocolate glaze – for those who want to up their cake game. Each is used daily in the studio and can be applied individually to other recipes.

The show-stopper element is in the assembly: three sections of sponge dabbed with orange syrup and layered with jam and milk chocolate cream. But it's not until you slice through the dark chocolate ganache and shimmering glaze that you realise what's inside.

Preheat the oven to 180°C fan-forced (200°C conventional). Spray an 18cm round cake tin with canola spray and dust with cocoa powder. Cut out a 16cm-diameter cake card.

For the chocolate sponge, add the egg yolks and glucose to the bowl of a stand mixer and whisk on medium speed until combined. Continue to whisk while adding the eggs one at a time until incorporated. Whisk until thick, about 3 minutes. Remove the bowl from the mixer.

Add the egg whites to a second bowl and whisk on medium speed until frothy. Gradually add the caster sugar and whisk to stiff peaks – don't over-beat. Fold the meringue into the first mixture.

Combine the remaining ingredients in a medium bowl, ensuring that there are no lumps. Gently fold the dry ingredients into the egg mixture until incorporated. Pour into the prepared tin and bake for about 25 minutes until cooked. Cool the cake in the tin for 15 minutes before turning out onto a wire rack. Refrigerate the cake to cool.
→

Orange syrup

75g caster sugar

zest of ½ orange

For the orange syrup, add 100g of water to a small saucepan, followed by the sugar and orange zest. Bring to a gentle simmer and stir to dissolve the sugar. Strain the syrup and store in an airtight container in the refrigerator until ready to use.

Milk chocolate cream

275g thickened cream, divided into a 100g portion and a 175g portion

175g milk chocolate, chopped

For the milk chocolate cream, heat the 100g portion of cream in a small saucepan until just under the boil.

Add the chocolate to a medium bowl and pour over the hot cream. Stand for 20 seconds before stirring to melt the chocolate. Once all the chocolate has melted and you have a smooth cream, add the 175g portion of cream and mix until thoroughly combined. Refrigerate for a minimum of 4 hours and a maximum of days. When ready to use, whisk to a piping consistency.

Shiny chocolate glaze

180g caster sugar

60g cocoa powder

105g thickened cream

11g gold-strength gelatine leaves, soaked in cold water

For the shiny chocolate glaze, add the sugar to a large bowl and sift in the cocoa powder. Add 140g of water and stir to make a paste. Add to a large, heavy-based saucepan with the cream. Place over medium heat and bring the mixture to the boil, stirring constantly. Boil while stirring for 1 minute. Remove the pan from the heat.

Lift the gelatine out of the water and squeeze out any excess water with your hands. Add the gelatine to the pan and stir well to dissolve. Strain the mixture through a sieve into a plastic container. Bubbles may appear on the surface of the glaze, but wait until the glaze has cooled right down before skimming the surface well with a spoon. Refrigerate the glaze, covered, until ready to use.

To assemble the cake, ensure that the sponge is chilled before cutting horizontally into three even layers. Use the top piece as the base and invert it to have the baked face down on the cake card. The flat base of the cake will be used for the top.

Heat the orange syrup and dab onto the sponge pieces to moisten each layer. Spread the jam liberally on the top of the bottom and middle layers of sponge.

Whip the milk chocolate cream until a piping consistency. Using 150g total for the bottom sponge, spread a little of the cream on the jam, add the remainder to the middle and push with a spatula almost to the edge, leaving a 1cm border around the cake. Place the middle sponge on top of the chocolate cream with the jam facing up. Repeat the chocolate cream step and place the top layer of sponge on the cream with the baked side facing up. Push down gently to flatten. Refrigerate the cake for a minimum of 2 hours to set.

Chocolate covering

375g thickened cream

40g liquid glucose

340g dark chocolate, chopped

125g unsalted butter

For the chocolate covering, add the cream and glucose to a small saucepan and bring to just under the boil.

Add the chocolate and butter to a medium bowl and pour over the hot cream. Stand for 30 seconds before stirring to a smooth, shiny cream. Cool at room temperature until thick enough to spread with a palette knife.

To assemble, remove the cake from the fridge and use a spatula or palette knife to smear and smooth the chocolate covering over the top and sides of the cake. Be fairly generous and try to smooth the sides as best you can. Place the cake in the freezer for 2 hours. Spoon any remaining covering into a piping bag to decorate the cake with.

Melt the glaze in the microwave in short bursts, stirring gently, until fluid. Don't whisk, as this will create air bubbles in the glaze. Set aside to cool. Use a thermometer to check the temperature of the glaze – if the glaze is too hot it will melt the cake, but too cold and it won't pour smoothly – and once it reaches 40°C, it's ready to use.

Remove the cake from the freezer and place on top of a tin or small stand – do this on a tray to catch the excess glaze. Pour the glaze over the cake, ensuring that it is entirely covered. Allow the glaze to finish dripping before cleaning the bottom edges of the cake of any excess drips with a palette knife. The glaze can be re-used by simply reheating, if needed, or refrigerated to use at a later date.

Lift the cake onto a serving plate and pipe neat bulbs of the remaining chocolate covering around the edges. Leave the cake plain, or finish it with berries, nuts or chocolate and serve immediately.

CRÈME BRÛLÉE

Vanilla Crème Brûlée
The Brûlée Cart

Makes 6

600ml thickened cream

1 vanilla pod, split lengthways, seeds scraped

6 extra-large egg yolks

½ cup caster sugar

6 raspberries

You have to admit that as far as portable food concepts go, a crème brûlée cart is as niche as it gets. The seed was planted when owners Jack and Bart White established a Belgian waffle cart with a $3000 loan from their great-grandfather. Their first gig was at an event at Hanging Rock and they paid back the loan that same day. The brothers were 15 and 13 years old respectively.

'There are only four ingredients, but you need to use them well,' says Jack. It's crucial that vanilla beans are used instead of essence, otherwise you risk what Jack refers to as 'that fake bakery taste'. He swears by Bulla cream, which is always consistent and is also Victorian. The sugar is from Bundaberg and the free-range eggs from Meggles farm.

'All the theatre is done in the torching and the garnishing,' says Jack. When blow-torching a crème brûlée, the trick is to do it as quickly and evenly as possibly. Do it in a circular motion and try not to go over the same spot twice. Those without a blowtorch can use an oven grill, but the latter has a tendency to melt the custard base instead of just the top layer of sugar.

This recipe will need to be started the day before serving. You will need a blowtorch for best results, but a hot grill will suffice.

Preheat the oven to 150°C fan-forced (170°C conventional). Line the base of a deep baking tray with a tea towel and place six 170ml ramekins on top.

Add the cream and vanilla pod and seeds to a medium saucepan over medium heat. Turn off the heat when the cream just begins to boil.

Meanwhile, whisk the egg yolks and ¼ cup of sugar in a medium bowl until pale. Gradually pour in the cream while whisking continuously. Once combined, add the mixture to the pan over medium–low heat. Stir constantly until thick enough to coat the back of a spoon, about 8 minutes. Do not boil the custard. Strain the custard through a fine sieve into a large jug and divide evenly between the ramekins. Carefully pour boiling water into the tray to reach halfway up the sides of the ramekins. Bake for about 30 minutes until the custard is firm around the edge. Remove the ramekins from the bain-marie and set aside to cool. Cover and refrigerate overnight.

When ready to serve, generously sprinkle the top of each crème brûlée with the remaining sugar and either caramelise with a blowtorch or under a hot grill. Top each brûlée with a raspberry and serve immediately.

Lime Panna Cotta with Tropical Fruit Salad, Banana and Passionfruit Sorbet and Coconut Popcorn
Philippa Sibley

Serves 6

½ mango, sliced

¼ small pineapple, peeled and sliced

½ perfect banana, sliced into rounds

3 passionfruit, pulp removed

1 pawpaw, balled with a melon baller

2 kiwifruit, peeled and quartered

mint leaves, to serve

Panna cotta

160g caster sugar

1 lime, washed and dried

650ml milk

5 gold-strength gelatine leaves, soaked in very cold water

350g sheep's milk yoghurt (or any plain yoghurt if sheep's milk isn't available)

Banana and passionfruit sorbet

140g caster sugar

25g liquid glucose

200ml passionfruit juice (pulp from 15 passionfruit – with the nodules where the seeds join the pith as well, as they give the colour – blended and pushed through a sieve. Make up any volume difference with orange juice)

300g perfectly ripe banana flesh (about 3 bananas), chopped

Coconut popcorn

50g caster sugar

50g popped popcorn

25g coconut flakes

Perhaps surprisingly – given her patisserie chef status earned from stints at Il Fornaio, Albert St Food & Wine and, most recently, The Hotel Windsor – Philippa Sibley doesn't have a sweet tooth. She's a savoury girl and besides, contact with flour causes her skin to erupt in an allergic reaction. 'When I get flour on me I break out. I have an obsessive aversion to having sticky fingers and I don't like sweets,' she says. 'I love tang and I love acidity. I love fruit-driven desserts.'

This lime panna cotta is a relatively new recipe in her repertoire, inspired by a breakfast she had in Thailand at the start of 2014; a milk jelly flavoured with loads of lime and served with tropical fruit. 'I normally add gold dust [an edible cake decoration that brings a metallic sparkle to dishes] to it. It looks amazing; like a tropical sunset.'

The banana and passionfruit sorbet accompaniment is one of Sibley's favourite recipes from her time working in France in the mid '90s. Not usually a fan of bananas ('they have to be perfectly ripe') their addition in this case gives the zingy sorbet an unusually creamy texture. In fact, she likes it so much, she wrote in her recipe notes to us, 'Best sorbet ever! Why am I giving the recipe away?'.

As far as panna cotta goes, the recipe is foolproof: setting it in glass means you don't have to rely on it holding its shape once it's turned out. 'It can be quite under-set and it's incredibly delicate, which is lovely ... It's a good base panna cotta that goes with any kind of fruit. It's amazing with berries like raspberries or strawberries, or citrus fruit in the middle of winter; blood orange, pink grapefruit and mandarin would be beautiful as well,' says Sibley.

You will need a candy thermometer for this recipe.

For the panna cotta, add the sugar to a small bowl and finely grate in the lime zest. Juice the lime, strain and set aside. Rub the zest into the sugar to make the most of the citrus oils and add to a medium saucepan with the milk. Bring to the boil and turn off the heat.

Lift the gelatine out of the water and squeeze out any excess water with your hands. Add the gelatine to the milk and swirl the pan to dissolve. Set aside to cool a little.

Add the yoghurt to a medium bowl and strain the cooled milk mix over the top. Add the lime juice and combine until smooth. Pour into six dessert glasses and refrigerate for at least 4 hours.

→

For the sorbet, add the sugar, glucose and 250ml of water to a small saucepan and bring to the boil. Cool before adding the passionfruit juice.

Spread the banana out in a small 3cm-deep tray. Pour the cooled syrup over the top and freeze until solid, about 2–3 hours.

Break up the frozen mixture and blitz in a food processor until fluffy. Freeze again for another 2 hours.

Line a baking tray with baking paper.

For the coconut popcorn, combine the sugar with 50ml of water in a small, heavy-based saucepan. Brush the side down with a clean pastry brush dipped in cold water and place over medium heat. Cook undisturbed, without stirring or swirling, until it reaches 121°C. Tip in the popcorn and coconut and mix well over low heat until the mixture dries and sounds crunchy. This will take a few minutes. Spread out on the prepared tray and set aside to cool. Store in an airtight container until needed.

To serve, gently mix the fruit together and divide between the glasses. Using a spoon dipped in hot water, top each with a big scoop of sorbet. Sprinkle with the popcorn and a few mint leaves and serve immediately.

224A Gertrude Street
Fitzroy

Tiramisu
Ladro

Serves 8–10

- 10 eggs, at room temperature
- 260g caster sugar
- 1kg mascarpone
- 1½ tablespoons marsala
- 36 savoiardi (lady finger biscuits)
- 500ml espresso coffee (or extra-strong plunger or percolated)
- 3 tablespoons good-quality raw cocoa powder
- 200g good-quality dark chocolate (Ladro uses Callebaut brand)
- 3 tablespoons chocolate-coated popping candy (or regular popping candy)

Ingrid Langtry and Sean Kierce have learned a lot since they first opened Ladro in 2003. They had to teach their little ones that you can't order dinner from a menu at home and that they should never, ever take tiramisu off the menu. 'We had people ring up and say, "Is it back on yet? We're not coming back in until it's on". They hold you at ransom,' says Langtry.

Valrhona or Callebaut chocolate is grated over the top, each one is sprinkled with dark chocolate-coated popping candy imported from Europe, and the dessert is made fresh each day so they remain aerated and fluffy. 'It does tend to thicken up when you refrigerate it overnight,' explains Langtry, who also recommends draining the coffee from the biscuits on a wire rack lined with paper towel.

Experimentation is also encouraged, from adding Montenegro or Italian bitters into the mixture instead of marsala, to soaking the biscuits in bitter orange sugar syrup instead of coffee. This recipe was passed down to former business partner and chef Rita Macali from her great grandmother.

Add the eggs to a large bowl (it must be clean and completely dry) and mix with an electric mixer on full speed for 5 minutes. Add the sugar and keep mixing on full speed for 3 minutes. By this stage the mixture should have doubled in size.

Turn the mixer off and gently whisk in the mascarpone by hand.

Start mixing again with an electric mixer on the lowest speed. Increase the speed every 2 minutes until you reach medium speed and the mixture has become very light and fluffy.

Turn the mixer off and very gently fold in the marsala with a spatula. Be careful not to be too aggressive, as the mix will lose its aeration.

Dip the savoiardi into the coffee quickly and place on a plate lined with paper towel. You don't want the biscuits too soggy or wet, as all the liquid will go to the bottom.

Layer individual jars or a large shallow dish (about 30cm x 25cm) with a little mascarpone mixture, some dipped savoiardi and a very light dusting of sifted cocoa. Repeat, then top with a layer of the mascarpone mixture, leaving enough room for the chocolate topping. Scrape the dark chocolate into curls with the edge of a spoon or using a vegetable peeler. Sprinkle the scraped chocolate and popping candy on top. Ladro likes to top it with as much as they can fit in the jar.

130 Acland Street
St Kilda

Sticky Date Pudding
Cicciolina

Makes 6

- 175g pitted dates
- 1 teaspoon bicarbonate of soda
- 85g unsalted butter, at room temperature
- 120g caster sugar
- 2 x 70g eggs
- 150g self-raising flour
- flaked almonds, to serve
- icing sugar, for dusting
- vanilla ice cream, to serve

Butterscotch sauce

- 110g unsalted butter
- 430g brown sugar
- 700ml thickened cream

Affectionately known as Cicc (pronounced 'chich') to those who frequent it, there's something immediately comfortable about stepping off Acland Street into Cicciolina. This is embedded in everything from the hospitality to the food. 'As a chef you think people would try the more complicated desserts,' says executive chef and co-owner Virginia Redmond, 'but they order what they're most comfortable with. That's why it's called comfort food; it sends them on their merry way feeling full and satisfied.'

Adapted from a banana pudding recipe she brought down from Noosa, this sticky date pudding has been on the menu for 20 years. Adults who came in as children eat it and then come back with dates and then again when they're engaged. After a couple of decades, the only major change to the recipe is that it's now plated up individually instead of being sliced from a cake front of house. Regulars even swing by to take it away for special occasions. Redmond recommends measuring and weighing all the ingredients before starting – to ensure you don't miss any steps.

Preheat the oven to 140°C fan-forced (160°C conventional). Grease six 180ml ramekins and dust with flour.

Add the dates and 90ml of water to a small saucepan and bring to the boil. Add the bicarbonate of soda and stir through, then remove from the heat and set aside for 5 minutes.

Cream the butter and caster sugar in a large bowl or using a stand mixer. Add one egg and mix until incorporated before incorporating the other egg.

Add the date mixture and butter mixture to a large bowl and, once combined, fold in the flour.

Pour the mixture into the prepared ramekins until about three-quarters full (don't overfill) and bake for 35–40 minutes.

To make the butterscotch sauce, melt the butter in a large saucepan over medium heat. Add the sugar and stir until combined. Cook for a few minutes, add the cream and bring to a full boil. Boil for 3½–4 minutes. Keep warm or heat through to serve.

Unmould the puddings onto plates, garnish with the almonds, dust with the icing sugar and serve with the butterscotch sauce and ice cream.

351 Lygon Street
Brunswick East

Chocolate and Hazelnut Ice Cream Sundae
Monsieur Truffe

Serves 8

Vanilla ice cream

500ml full-cream milk

500ml thickened cream

2 vanilla pods, split lengthways, seeds scraped

200g egg yolks (about 10)

200g caster sugar

Chewy choc brownie

360g Monsieur Truffe chocolate (70% cocoa), chopped

200g butter, diced

4 eggs

200g caster sugar

200g plain flour

1 teaspoon baking powder

20g cacao nibs

Hazelnut praline

100g caster sugar

50g hazelnuts, roasted, peeled and chopped

Chocolate hazelnut sauce

1 cup hazelnuts, roasted and peeled

3 tablespoons Monsieur Truffe dark cocoa powder

½ cup raw sugar

1 pinch of salt flakes

80ml hazelnut oil

Kids have been known to leave their Monsieur Truffe hot chocolates unfinished at East Elevation, the cafe that houses the Monsieur Truffe chocolate factory. But chef and co-owner Brian Edwards has come up with a solution especially for this cookbook: add ice cream. 'We do have some chocolate that kids turn their noses up at because it is quite strong; they're used to Milo and Cadbury,' explains Edwards. 'But because this has the vanilla ice cream it's not quite as full on. Ice cream makes everything taste good; it's appreciated by all age groups.'

Aside from the ice cream, made with real vanilla and full-cream milk, the chocolate has been incorporated into a chewy brownie (sold on its own at East Elevation) and hazelnut sauce. The former uses Monsieur Truffe's 70 per cent range, a single-origin Ecuadorian chocolate sourced from France, while the latter incorporates dark chocolate powder. Add hazelnut praline for a bit of crunch and it's a dessert to please the masses.

Purchasing Monsieur Truffe's dark chocolate and hazelnut spread is a fine alternative to making your own. If making for the kids, Edwards suggests omitting the cacao nibs. 'They're a nice balance against the sweetness, but are naturally quite bitter.'

You will need an ice cream machine for this recipe.

Preheat the oven to 180°C fan-forced (200°C conventional). Line a 20cm x 30cm baking tray with baking paper.

For the ice cream, add the milk, cream and vanilla pod and seeds to a medium saucepan and bring to a simmer.

Meanwhile, whisk the egg yolks and sugar in a large bowl until pale and thick. Pour a third of the hot milk into the egg mix while whisking continuously. Pour this mixture into the milk in the pan and place over medium heat. Stir constantly with a wooden spatula until thickened – don't let it boil or get too hot or it will scramble. It's ready when you can run your finger over the back of the spoon and the line remains distinct. Alternatively, use a thermometer and bring the mix up to 80°C. To halt the cooking, strain into a steel bowl resting in an ice bath. Continue stirring as it cools. Churn the ice cream according to the manufacturer's instructions.

→

For the brownie, melt 300g of the chocolate in a large stainless steel bowl over a saucepan of simmering water. Add the butter and stir to combine. Take off the heat but keep warm.

Add the eggs and sugar to a large bowl and whisk with an electric mixer until pale and creamy, about 4–5 minutes. Fold into the warm chocolate and butter mixture. Sift in the flour and baking powder and fold through. Gently stir in the remaining chocolate and the cacao nibs until combined. Pour into the prepared tray and bake for 15–20 minutes until lightly puffed and springy to the touch – the top should be shiny and slightly cracked. Cool in the tray before turning out.

For the praline, add the sugar and hazelnuts to a small saucepan over medium heat, stir to coat the nuts and caramelise gently. Once a medium caramel, pour the mixture out onto a non-stick baking sheet, spread out evenly and set aside to cool. Once cooled and set, smash the praline into pieces with a toffee hammer or rolling pin.

For the sauce, blitz the hazelnuts in a high-powered food processor until a smooth butter, about 3 minutes. Add the remaining ingredients and continue blending until smooth and creamy.

To assemble the sundaes, break off pieces of brownie and drop into glasses or jars. Drizzle generously with the sauce, sprinkle over some praline and add a scoop of ice cream. Follow with more brownie pieces, more hazelnut sauce, more praline and more ice cream.

299 Lygon Street
Carlton

Nutella Swirl Gelato
Pidapipó

Makes about 1 litre

515g full-cream milk

28g egg yolk

105g caster sugar

35g dextrose or fructose powder

½ teaspoon carob powder

25g skim milk powder

128g cream, divided into an 80g portion and a 48g portion

80g condensed milk

80g Nutella, plus extra to serve

waffle cones, to serve

Lisa Valmorbida is a chef and graduate of Carpigiani Gelato University, a niche institute teaching students bona fide gelati-making methods in Bologna. After finishing the course in 2012, Valmorbida visited Vicenza, her family's hometown, where she worked in a local gelateria. It reminded her of growing up with her Italian nonno, who had introduced her to gelato and the game Pidapipó, an Italian version of Simon Says.

Pidapipó the gelateria started as a pop-up shop around the corner from its current spot on Faraday Street. There, Valmorbida trialled different flavours, including this Nutella Swirl Gelato. 'When we had the pop-up it was so popular we decided to put a Nutella tap in at Lygon Street,' she says. Part of the appeal is that the Nutella remains gooey in the gelato instead of crystallising and hardening like melted chocolate.

Valmorbida has altered this recipe for a domestic kitchen. For example, she doesn't normally use egg yolks, instead sourcing plant-based emulsifiers and thickeners. 'When freezing it, the faster it freezes the smoother the texture will be,' she says. 'Put the mixture in the freezer for 30 minutes before you put it in the churner.'

You will need a candy or probe thermometer and a gelato or ice cream machine for this recipe.

Add the milk and egg yolk to a large stainless steel bowl over a saucepan of simmering water, taking care to ensure that the bowl doesn't touch the water. Whisk continuously while slowly adding the sugar and the dextrose or fructose, carob and skim milk powders. Once all the dry ingredients have been added, continue whisking until the mixture reaches 80°C. Remove the bowl from the heat and whisk in 80g of cream until combined.

Strain the mixture through a fine sieve into a container and cool in the fridge for a few hours. Once the mixture is cool, add the condensed milk and the remaining cream and blend together with a hand-held blender until a rich, even consistency. Place the mixture in the freezer for 30 minutes, then add the mixture to the ice-cream machine and churn according to the manufacturer's instructions.

In a stainless steel bowl over simmering water, gently heat the Nutella until just fluid. Drizzle the Nutella into the machine immediately before transferring the gelato to the freezer. Freeze for 2–3 hours until firm.

To serve, scoop the gelato into waffle cones and drizzle over a little melted Nutella.

55–57 Gertrude Street
Fitzroy

Chocolate Honeycomb Terrine
Cutler & Co.

Serves 8–10

200g dark couverture chocolate, chopped

100g unsalted butter, chopped

4 egg yolks

70g vanilla sugar

2 teaspoons Dutch cocoa powder

2 tablespoons almond meal

2 egg whites

1 pinch of salt flakes

40g caster sugar

150g honeycomb, broken

whipped cream, to serve

All desserts have a 'good bit', whether it's the filling of a doughnut or the outside of a Golden Gaytime. One of the advantages of being a chef is that you can recreate the good bit and use it in other dishes. That's exactly what happened with this chocolate terrine from Andrew McConnell.

'The actual chocolate terrine itself was taken from a recipe I used to use for a chocolate tart,' says McConnell. 'I really liked the filling and thought it didn't need the pastry, so I baked it and luckily it worked. It's pretty silken and it develops a subtle crust on the top when you turn it out. It's quite a luxurious finish and not too dense, which is what I like about it.'

McConnell refers to the chocolate terrine as a 'base recipe', saying additions and substitutions such as hazelnuts, pralines and spices can be used. 'I've added cinnamon, clove and cardamom to it, which is really nice, and a little bit of orange zest that really plays on the chocolate,' he says. The recipe can be cooked a couple of days in advance and will keep in the fridge, perfect for those who want to pre-prepare.

Preheat the oven to 130°C fan-forced (150°C conventional). Butter an 8cm x 18cm 750ml terrine mould. Line the base and short sides with a strip of baking paper extending 2cm beyond the rim of the terrine – this will make it easier to unmould.

Add the chocolate and butter to a stainless steel bowl set over a saucepan of simmering water. Once mostly melted, stir to combine and take off the heat.

Meanwhile, whisk the egg yolks and vanilla sugar in a large bowl until thick and pale.

Sift the cocoa into a small bowl. Run your fingers through the almond meal to break up any lumps and combine with the cocoa.

Add the egg whites and a pinch of salt to a large bowl and whisk to soft peaks with an electric mixer. Gradually add the caster sugar, a teaspoon at a time, whisking until incorporated. Whisk for a further minute to completely dissolve the sugar.

→

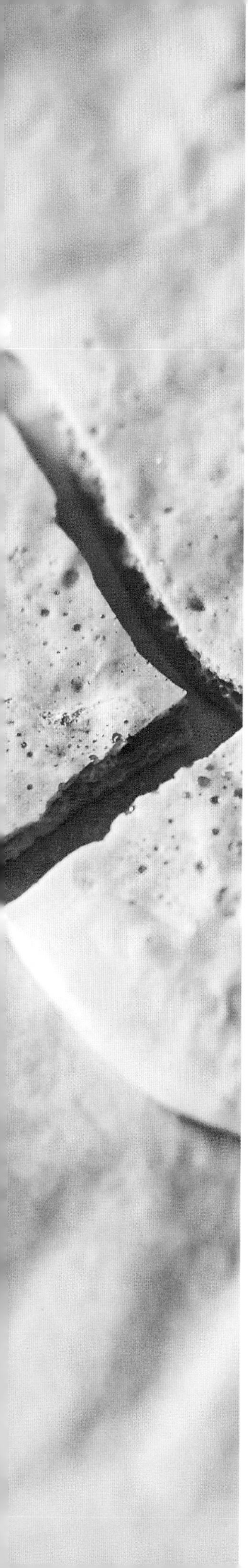

Fold the warm chocolate mixture into the egg yolk mixture, and then quickly stir in the cocoa and almond meal. Fold in the meringue with a large metal spoon. Spoon the mix into the prepared terrine mould and cover with a piece of greased foil.

Place the terrine in a small deep baking tray and pour in enough boiling water to reach halfway up the sides of the mould. Bake for 30 minutes, reduce the temperature to 100°C fan-forced (120°C conventional) and bake for a further 15 minutes. Once cooked, remove the terrine from the tray and cool to room temperature. Refrigerate for 4 hours.

To serve, run a hot palette knife around the edge of the terrine and turn it out onto a platter. Top the terrine with the broken honeycomb, slice with a hot knife and serve with the whipped cream.

Level 55 Rialto Towers
525 Collins Street
Melbourne

Barbecued Mango with Lime, Coconut and White Chocolate
Vue de Monde

Serves 8

4 ripe mangos, cheeks sliced off, skin on

lime zest, to serve

edible leaves and flowers, to serve

White chocolate powder

100g white chocolate, chopped

1 lime, washed and dried

Lime curd

1 gold-strength gelatine leaf

100ml lime juice

2 eggs

3 tablespoons caster sugar

40g unsalted butter, cubed

Mango sorbet

1 gold-strength gelatine leaf

100g caster sugar

50g light corn syrup

300g mango puree (flesh of 2–3 ripe mangos, blended)

Candied coconut

1 egg white

2 tablespoons caster sugar

1 teaspoon vanilla essence (or seeds from ½ vanilla pod)

1 pinch of salt flakes

1½ cups desiccated coconut

'The idea was produce driven,' explains Vue de Monde's head pastry chef, John Demetrios. 'We had a look at what was coming in and spoke with suppliers and the Aussie mangos had just come into season.'

The team had to fulfil both the restaurant's taste and theatre requirements with the new dish, where an element of it must be prepared at the table. The result: a good, old-fashioned barbecue. Fresh mango is grilled flesh-side down, spread with mango sorbet and decorated with lime curd, crispy coconut and sea salt. Vue de Monde adds chamomile powder, but the white chocolate and lime crumb substituted here uses more accessible ingredients.

'At home, the idea is that you can have a barbecue on a hot day, put a few mangos on, and by the time you've eaten they've cooled down and are ready to go,' says Demetrios. He adds that it's essential to use ripe mangos that are already sweet. When mangos aren't in season, figs work well, too.

You will need an ice cream machine for this recipe.

For the white chocolate powder, add the white chocolate to a medium stainless steel bowl and place over a saucepan of barely simmering water, ensuring that the bowl never touches the water. Remove the bowl once the chocolate has mostly melted and stir briefly until smooth. Finely grate in the zest from the lime and stir to combine. Pour into a container about 7cm x 15cm and freeze until solid – the size isn't critical here, but you want to form a block that is easy to grate.

For the lime curd, add the gelatine to a small bowl of ice-cold water and set aside for 5 minutes until soft and pliable. Remove from the water, squeeze out any excess water with your hands and set aside.

Add the lime juice, eggs and caster sugar to a medium stainless steel bowl set over a saucepan of barely simmering water. Whisk until the mixture thickens or is over 82°C and take off the heat. Stir the gelatine and butter through the mix and tip into a blender. Process until smooth, strain into a container and refrigerate until completely cool.

→

For the mango sorbet, add the gelatine to a small bowl of ice-cold water and set aside for 5 minutes until soft and pliable. Remove from the water, squeeze out any excess water with your hands and set aside.

Bring 100g of water, the sugar and corn syrup to the boil in a small saucepan. Turn off the heat, add the gelatine and stir until dissolved.

Combine the sugar syrup with the mango puree and refrigerate until completely cold. Churn in an ice cream machine according to the manufacturer's instructions. Freeze until required.

Preheat the oven to 160°C fan-forced (180°C conventional). Line a baking tray with baking paper.

For the candied coconut, whisk the egg white, sugar, vanilla and salt in a medium bowl until combined. Fold through the coconut and spread out on the prepared tray. Roast for about 15 minutes, stirring through every 5 minutes, until evenly golden. Leftover candied coconut will keep for up to 2 weeks in an airtight container.

Grill the mango cheeks, flesh-side down, for 1–2 minutes on a hot barbecue or in a griddle pan. Set aside to cool.

Spread 2 tablespoons of sorbet on top of each mango cheek. Fill a piping bag with the lime curd and pipe five dots, about the size of a 10-cent coin, on top of the sorbet. Sprinkle 3 teaspoons of the candied coconut crumble over the top, grate 3 teaspoons of white chocolate over each mango, garnish with a little lime zest, top with the edible flowers and leaves and serve immediately.

Old Fashioned

421 Rathdowne Street
Carlton

Drinks for After Dinner
with Dave Kerr of The Beaufort

Traditionally, a digestif is an alcoholic beverage taken after dinner to aid digestion. It's largely a European ritual (the Italians have grappa; the Portuguese port; the Spanish sherry) but it never caught on down under in the same way. More recently, an invigoration of the digestif has been seen locally with the emergence of gin and vermouth bars in Melbourne, but of course the after-dinner drink should be enjoyed at home in the company of others too.

Bartender Dave Kerr, of The Beaufort in Carlton, provides us with some pairing and recipe suggestions so you can keep drinking after dessert.

A few tips:

Chill your glassware. It will keep your drinks cool longer and enhance the experience.

Make garnishes using a Y or potato peeler, but don't peel too close to the pith, as it will add bitterness to your drink. And be careful with your fingers when peeling.

To make a sugar syrup, mix equal parts caster sugar to hot water, measuring both by weight for accuracy. Stir together until the liquid is clear. Keep in the fridge for up to 1 week.

Beer and Whisky Matching

There always seems to be a three-quarter full bottle of whisky in every home. It's such a good default. Add beer and it becomes what's commonly referred to as a Boilermaker. Try matching Highland Scotch whisky – an easier drinking style on the sweeter side, characterised by honey, heathers, deep chocolate and raisin – with a rich, dark beer. Kerr's preference is Glenfarclas 15, which he says tastes a little like Christmas cake. Try mixing it with something like Holgate's Temptress, a chocolate porter-style beer perfect for filling the dessert part of your stomach and giving you a little buzz.

For those who prefer finishing with something more savoury, a smoky whisky from the islands brings finality to the palate. These whiskies can taste almost medicinal at times and have a similar effect to a herbal Amaro or other traditional Italian digestif. The Bunnahabhain 12 is a great place to start if you're not a huge whisky drinker, backed up with a bold Indian Pale Ale (IPA) to continue challenging the palate and round out the meal. Feral's Hop Hog IPA is an Aussie classic and it's hard to find a better example of an IPA made in Australia.

→

Death Flip

Serves 1

- 30ml Don Julio tequila
- 15ml Jägermeister
- 15ml yellow chartreuse
- 1 egg
- 10ml sugar syrup (see recipe on page 271)
- ice
- fresh nutmeg, to serve

This drink was created by Chris Hysted, Ketel One brand ambassador and one-time bartender at world-renowned Fitzroy bar Black Pearl. As a young bartender he was constantly trying to sneak his favourite ingredients into drinks, which at the time happened to be chartreuse and Jägermeister – arguably the two pillars of the complex digestif world. He put this drink on the menu, neglected to list the ingredients for fear of a backlash and people lost their minds over it. It's popped up on lists all over the world and has turned into a modern classic.

Dry-shake all the ingredients in a cocktail shaker (the lack of ice helps the egg break down and emulsify). Add ice to your shaker and give it another solid shake.

Strain into a chilled tumbler and grate a touch of nutmeg over the top.

Grasshopper

Serves 1

- 30ml creme de menthe
- 30ml cream
- 30ml creme de cacao
- ice
- chocolate, to serve

Drinks made with equal parts are a rarity in the cocktail world, but this is a great example. If you're not the world's biggest after-dinner mint fan, play around with a lesser amount of crème de menthe.

Quality crème de menthe is the key to turning this ironic, outdated drink into a delicious lost classic. Tamborine Mountain Distillery makes a great one, or seek out Joseph Cartron from a decent bottle shop.

Add all the ingredients to a cocktail shaker. Shake vigorously and strain into a cocktail or wine glass.

If you want to relive the '80s, get out the Microplane and shave some chocolate over the top.

Whisky Sour

Serves 1

- 60ml blended whisky
- 25ml freshly squeezed lemon juice
- 20ml sugar syrup (see recipe on page 271)
- 1 egg white
- ice

When serving this timeless cocktail, be sure to pick a decent blended Scotch whisky. Single malts are a bit of a waste here but Monkey Shoulder is always a good option.

Ice moulds can be found at cooking stores and online and make a huge difference to the finished product. The larger blocks of ice ensure a highly chilled drink and also reduce dilution that can turn the drink watery.

Add all the ingredients to a cocktail shaker, fill with ice and shake as hard as possible.

Strain the liquid into half of your shaker and discard the ice. Shake again, this time with no ice (this will allow the egg white to aerate and result in that signature fluffy head).

Strain the liquid over a large ice block in a rocks glass. Be sure to get as much of the egg white out of the shaker as possible.

Old Fashioned

Serves 1

- 10ml sugar syrup (see recipe on page 271)
- 5 dashes of Angostura bitters
- ice
- 60ml liquor (rye whisky, English-style rum if you have a sweet tooth, or even a shot of quality tequila)
- 1 orange, to serve

One of the oldest cocktails around, this is commonly made with a cube of bitters. Traditionally it takes a long time to stir down the drink (stirring to the point that the drink is at a consistent temperature) but most people don't have time for that.

Place the sugar syrup and bitters in the bottom of a solid rocks glass. Add two cubes of ice and 20ml liquor. Stir down for 7 rotations. Add two more cubes and 20ml liquor. Stir down for 7 rotations.

Fill the glass with ice and the remaining booze. Stir for 7 more rotations and then taste for balance, sweetness and dilution. Adjust accordingly if necessary, keeping in mind that the drink will dilute as you drink it, so make the assessment based on how strong you want it initially and how weak you want it to be at the end.

To garnish, take a long strip of peel from an orange and then hold the peel over the drink about 10cm above the rim. Using your thumb and middle finger, grip the edges of the peel and gently squeeze the aromatic oils over the drink. Push the garnish down the edge of the glass so that it's partly protruding – this way you get a good nose-full of orange every time you take a sip.

Coda, Melbourne

Baker D. Chirico, Carlton

Acknowledgements

To all who helped in the making of The Broadsheet Melbourne Cookbook, we'd like to thank you.

This cookbook has been an incredibly rewarding project to work on, made possible by the fantastic team involved.

Thank you to publisher Mary Small and project editor Clare Marshall at Plum, who we've co-published the book with. They've been essential at every turn, extremely supportive and great to collaborate with on our first book.

Thank you to editor Marcus Ellis for going through the recipes with a fine toothcomb and working with the chefs and recipe testers to make them accessible for home cooks.

Thank you to our writer Sofia Levin, who spoke to and wrote an introduction for every cafe, restaurant and bar we've included.

Thank you to The Company You Keep, our tireless design collaborators. Nothing would look so sharp without your eyes across every detail, Rhys Gorgol and Veronica Lethorn.

The Broadsheet team, it is from these foundations that the book was created, as an extension of what we do online everyday. Thank you.

It was a fantastic opportunity to work with photographer Mark Roper and his assistant Rich MacDonald. Together with stylist and recipe tester Deborah Kaloper, they were a dream team and made shooting 80 dishes in 70 venues a breeze.

Thank you to Andrew McConnell, who has written our foreword and been a supporter of Broadsheet's from the beginning.

Finally, a very special thank you to each and every restaurant involved. This book is about celebrating the best food and drink in Melbourne and we're so lucky to be able to do that. The trust each of them has shown by giving us the opportunity to represent them is enormous and we don't take that for granted.

We look forward to working with you all again soon.

Nick Shelton Publisher & Founder
Caroline Clements Publications Director

Food Supplier Directory

Butchers

Berties Butcher
218 Swan Street, Richmond
(03) 9428 2655
bertiesbutchers.com

The Butcher's Block
280 Queen Parade, Clifton Hill
(03) 9489 9225
butchersblock.ch

Cannings Free Range Butchers
100 Burwood Road, Hawthorn
16 Woodford Avenue, Kew
1300 513 623
canningsfreerangebutchers.com.au

Jonathan's
122 Smith Street, Collingwood
(03) 9419 4339
jonathans.com.au

Meatsmith
273 Smith Street, Fitzroy
meatsmith.com.au

Peter Bouchier
551 Malvern Road, Toorak
(03) 9827 3629
petergbouchier.com.au

Cheesemongers

La Formaggeria
70 Acland Street, St Kilda
(03) 9534 1111
laformaggeria.com.au

La Latteria
104 Elgin Street, Carlton
(03) 9347 9009
lalatteria.com.au

Milk the Cow
323 Lygon Street, Carlton
(03) 9348 4771
157 Fitzroy Street, St Kilda
(03) 9537 2225
milkthecow.com.au

Richmond Hill Larder
48-50 Bridge Road, Richmond
(03) 9421 2808
rhcl.com.au

Spring Street Grocer
157 Spring Street, Melbourne
(03) 9639 0335
springstreetgrocer.com.au

Delicatessens

Casa Iberica Deli
25 Johnston Street, Fitzroy
(03) 9419 4420
casaibericadeli.com.au

DOC Delicatessen
330 Lygon Street, Carlton
(03) 9347 8482
docgroup.net

The Essential Ingredient
Elizabeth Street, South Yarra
(03) 9827 9047
theessentialingredient.com.au

King & Godfree
293 Lygon Street, Carlton
(03) 9347 1619
kingandgodfree.com.au

Mediterranean Wholesalers
482 Sydney Road, Brunswick
(03) 9380 4777

Smith & Deli
111 Moor Street, Fitzroy
(03) 9042 4117

All of the chefs in this book reiterated the importance of using fresh, quality produce. Below are a few recommended suppliers where we suggest purchasing ingredients when making the dishes in this book.

Fishmongers

Canals Seafood
703 Nicholson Street,
Carlton North
(03) 9380 4537

Clamms Seafood
2 Somerville Road,
Yarraville
(03) 9689 6322
clamms.com.au

Ocean Made Seafood
25–29 Robert Street,
Collingwood
(03) 9486 0399
oceanmade.com.au

Greengrocers

The Leaf Store
111–113 Ormond Road,
Elwood
(03) 9531 6542
theleafstore.com.au

Plump Organic Grocery
24 Ballarat Street, Yarraville
(03) 9687 6422
plump.com.au

Ripe Organics
163 Commercial Road,
South Yarra
(03) 9804 8606
ripeorganics.com.au

Smith & Maloney
157 Lygon Street,
Brunswick East
(03) 9381 1416

St Clements
384 Rathdowne Street,
Carlton North
(03) 9347 8336

The Vegetable Connection
85 Victoria Street, Fitzroy
(03) 9417 3014
vegetableconnection.com.au

Markets

Coburg North Primary School Farmers Market
180 O'Hea Street, Coburg

Collingwood Children's Farm Farmers Market
18 St Heliers Street, Abbotsford

Dandenong Market
Corner of Clow and
Cleeland Streets, Dandenong
dandenongmarket.com.au

Prahran Market
163 Commercial Road,
South Yarra
prahranmarket.com.au

Preston Market
Corner of Cramer Street
and Murray Road, Preston
(03) 9478 3130

Queen Victoria Market
Corner of Victoria and
Elizabeth Streets, Melbourne
qvm.com.au

South Melbourne Market
Corner of Coventry and Cecil
Streets, South Melbourne
(03) 9209 6295
southmelbournemarket.com.au

Index

Q

R

S

Bar Di Stasio, St Kilda

Design The Company You Keep
Editing Marcus Ellis
Index Jo Rudd
Photography Mark Roper
Prop and food styling Deborah Kaloper
Typesetting Kirby Jones
Colour reproduction
Splitting Image Colour Studio

Printed and bound in China
1010 Printing International Limited

Back cover photo of
Supernormal by Mark Roper

A Plum and Broadsheet Media book

First published in 2015 by Pan Macmillan Australia Pty Limited
Level 25, 1 Market Street, Sydney, NSW 2000, Australia

Level 1, 15–19 Claremont Street, South Yarra, Victoria 3141, Australia

Recipes for Whole, Slow-Roasted Lamb Shoulder (page 214), Organic Carrots with Almond Cream and Harissa (page 215) and Tuna Tartare with Crushed Pea Salad (page 216) adapted with permission from Cumulus Inc. by Andrew McConnell, 2011, published by Lantern, an imprint of Penguin; Recipe for Pulpo a la Gallega (page 113) adapted with permission from MoVida: Spanish Culinary Adventures by Frank Camorra and Richard Cornish, 2007, published by Murdoch Books.

10 9 8 7 6